NO-NONSENSE
BUDDHISM
FOR BEGINNERS

NO-NONSENSE BUDDHISM
FOR BEGINNERS

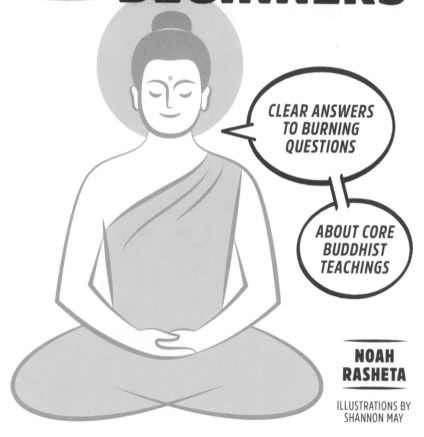

CLEAR ANSWERS
TO BURNING
QUESTIONS

ABOUT CORE
BUDDHIST
TEACHINGS

**NOAH
RASHETA**

ILLUSTRATIONS BY
SHANNON MAY

ALTHEA
PRESS

For my wife, Giselle.
Thank you for all your support.

For my children, Rajko, Noelle,
and Genevieve. May you see
beauty in the impermanent and
interdependent nature of all
things. I love you very much!

For my friend and teacher,
Koyo Kubose. Gasshō.

CONTENTS

HOW TO USE THIS BOOK

My journey with Buddhism began in 2010, when difficult times in my personal life led me to question everything I knew. I decided to seek comfort in meditation and Buddhism, but the more I learned, the more I realized there was no secret formula to eliminating discomfort in my life. It became clear that trying to eliminate suffering was actually causing me more suffering. I wanted to know more about this seeming paradox, so I started an in-depth study of Buddhist philosophy, devouring over 100 books on the subject. Soon, I started a local meditation group and began teaching Buddhist concepts to other people who were going through difficulties in life, like infidelity or religious disillusionment. Later, I started a successful podcast called *Secular Buddhism* and spent two years in a ministry program to become a Buddhist minister. Now I teach mindfulness and Buddhist philosophy online and in workshops all around the world.

This book is an introduction to Buddhism written for people who are trying to gain a basic understanding of Buddhist philosophy and core Buddhist teachings. By the end of this book, you should have a solid foundation of knowledge about Buddhism and its history. This groundwork will help you begin or continue your own Buddhist practice and understand Buddhism's ongoing cultural influence today, which can be seen in Western interest in meditation, the current "mindfulness craze," and the nearly 500 million Buddhist practitioners around the world.

Each of this book's four parts will help you gain a basic understanding of a different aspect of Buddhism, including who the Buddha was, how he viewed the world, what he taught, and how those teachings are put into practice over 2,500 years later by Buddhists and non-Buddhists alike.

The book is written in a question-and-answer format, and many of the questions here reflect inquiries I've gotten when I teach in-person workshops and seminars on Buddhism. Part 1 is centered on the historical figure known as the Buddha, while part 2 focuses on key Buddhist concepts and ideas you'll need to help you understand the Buddha's most significant teachings. Part 3 covers the teachings that are the basis of Buddhist philosophy and religious traditions. Finally, in part 4, we'll explore Buddhist practices, including things like meditation and chanting. Because of the way it's structured, newcomers to Buddhism will get the most out of this book by reading in order from start to finish. But you can also use it like a reference book—if you're interested in particular topics, you can find them in the index and go directly to those pages.

Throughout the book, you will see occasional sidebars from the main text labeled "Everyday Buddhism." In those sections, I try to bring the topics I'm discussing down to earth by giving you examples from everyday life. Some of these concepts can seem a little abstract, so my hope is that the stories I share will demonstrate how Buddhist teachings can reveal themselves in your day-to-day experience.

I want to make a quick note here about the different schools of Buddhism (we'll talk about this in more depth on page 22). If someone wrote a book called *No-Nonsense Christianity for Beginners*, there would be some significant differences if the author were a Catholic as opposed to, say, a Jehovah's Witness. Christianity is broad, and there are many differences in doctrine and approach among its various branches. The same is true for Buddhism. I personally started off studying Tibetan Buddhism, then shifted focus to Zen Buddhism. I later graduated from a ministry program that was heavily influenced by Pure Land Buddhism, but today I practice secular Buddhism. So, while I do my best here to give a neutral view regarding the relative merits of any specific tradition, I realize that I am inevitably influenced by the schools of Buddhism in which I've studied and learned these teachings. My hope is that you'll be able to gain a general overview of Buddhist ideas and teachings from this book, with the understanding that teachers in other traditions may have different ways of explaining some of these concepts.

And a note about language: It's common in Buddhism to hear the words *skillful* and *unskillful* being used when referring to aspects of the Buddhist path. This comes from the Sanskrit expression *upāya-kaushalya*, meaning "skill in means." *Skillful means* is a concept in Mahayana Buddhism that emphasizes that a Buddhist practitioner may use his or her own methods or techniques on the path to enlightenment depending on his or her own particular set of circumstances. The Buddha was known for adapting his teachings to the specific person or audience he was addressing, taking into account the listener's needs and skill level. In this way, we can adapt Buddhist practices to conform to our individual needs and circumstances. This is considered skillful means. Now let's start learning about Buddhism!

PART 1

THE BUDDHA

What You'll Learn: In this section, we'll discuss the figure Siddhartha Gautama, now known as the Buddha. You'll learn about his life and some of the key events that led to his enlightenment, as well as how his teachings developed into a philosophical system and, eventually, a world religion. Though several millennia old, the Buddha's teachings and philosophy are still relevant today.

Who was the Buddha? Was he a real person, or is he a myth?

Buddha is a title that was given to a man named Siddhartha Gautama. Siddhartha lived around 500 BCE in northern India and what is now Nepal. Generally, when people refer to "the Buddha," they're referring to Siddhartha, the man whose teachings became the foundation of what we now call Buddhism. There is little scholarly debate around Siddhartha's existence; however, there is some debate around specific events in his life. As is common with many ancient traditions, the original Buddhist teachings have evolved into teachings *about* the teachings. This opens up more room for individual teachers' interpretations but brings into question the historical accuracy of modern-day retellings. However, we can still tell a lot about the Buddha by his teachings that have been passed down.

We know that they center on two main themes: the problem of human suffering and the methods that can bring about the cessation of suffering. The Buddha taught a method of living intended to be practiced, rather than a set of ideas he asked his followers to believe. His teachings, known collectively as the *dharma*, invite us to look inward and study our own minds in order to gain a clearer understanding of ourselves and of the nature of reality.

What language did the Buddha speak? I often hear foreign-sounding words used to describe things in Buddhism—is that the Buddha's original language?

It's likely that the Buddha would have spoken Māgadhī Prākrit, the spoken language of the ancient Māgadha kingdom in northern India. But we can't say that with total certainty, as there is no written record of his teachings in his native language. During his lifetime and for a long while after, his teachings were transmitted orally across India and modern-day Nepal. It wasn't until several hundred years after the Buddha's death that the teachings were finally collected and written down. One of the oldest collections of his written teachings is known as the Pali Canon because it's written in Pali, a language once used for academic and religious purposes in India. Since that's the oldest known source of many of these teachings, you will notice many Pali words being used in this book and in many other writings about Buddhism. Also common are words in Sanskrit, a language closely related to Pali and still used as a liturgical language in India.

What do we know about the historical Buddha? What led him to his moment of enlightenment?

The traditional story is that Siddhartha Gautama was born in Lumbini, in what is now Nepal, sometime around 500 BCE. He was the son of a king, raised in luxury and affluence. By the age of 29, he was married, had a son, and was carrying out his princely duties when, one day, everything changed. While on a carriage ride outside the palace, he encountered first an old man, then a sick person, and then a corpse. Up until this point, Siddhartha had lived a sheltered life in the palace and had been shielded from the realities of old age, sickness, and death. These encounters shook him to the core. He realized that his affluence and luxury would not protect him from suffering and mortality, and it troubled him deeply. Siddhartha then noticed a mendicant monk—a wandering spiritual seeker who begged and relied on charitable donations to survive while he sought spiritual wisdom. This monk seemed peaceful and serene; he didn't appear to feel troubled the way Siddhartha did. Siddhartha was inspired to seek this spiritual wisdom in order to ease his discomfort about the harsh realities of life.

Siddhartha renounced the life of a prince and began his quest for inner peace. He worked with gurus and teachers who practiced extreme forms of self-control and asceticism. After six years of devoted study and spiritual practice ranging from meditation to long periods of fasting, Siddhartha felt frustrated that he still wasn't getting the answers to his questions or gaining the wisdom he sought. He eventually realized that the path to peace was to be found through mental discipline. At a site in northern India, he sat in meditation under a fig tree, where he wrestled with his own mind, struggling with the concepts and ideas that were blinding him from seeing reality clearly. After seven days, he suddenly understood that he was the source of his own discomfort and suffering, as well as the source of the joy and contentment he so desperately sought. Upon realizing that the wisdom he sought was to be found within himself rather than outside himself, he attained enlightenment. He would come to be known as the Buddha, from the Pali and Sanskrit word for "awakened." The site at which he reached enlightenment would become known as Bodh Gaya and that tree as the Bodhi tree, in his honor.

Reality vs. Our Perception of Reality

Imagine you're driving on the freeway when suddenly a car cuts into your lane, forcing you to slam on the brakes. A common reaction is to honk your horn or show that driver a certain finger. You may even experience that powerful surge of anger we call road rage. Why do we tend to become angry, even furious, in moments like these?

From the Buddhist perspective, our perception of the reality of any situation (in this case, a car cutting us off) is influenced as much by ideas as it is by what actually happened. In this scenario, we might think, "This jerk cut me off!" But the idea that the other driver is a selfish, mean person who cut us off intentionally is a fictional narrative we created in our own mind. How do we know this person is a jerk? What if he or she just got devastating news and was distracted because of it? What if he or she was having a medical emergency? Would any of those scenarios alter the feelings you experienced in this scenario? Probably so. The reality of the situation is that a car cut you off, and that's all you know. Everything else is uncertain; we don't know who the driver is, why he or she behaved that way, or what is going on in that car.

In our day-to-day lives, we're continually making meaning and creating stories about everything that happens. A thought arises, we create a story about it, the story evokes an emotion, we create another story about that, and on and on until, before we know it, we're hardly paying attention to our lived reality at all, trapped in a habitual reactivity to our own thoughts.

Buddhist teachings can give us a new perspective. Our stories sometimes seem to comfort us because they give us a sense of certainty, even when they're not true. But there is great freedom in releasing ourselves from the stories that cloud our perceptions and starting to feel okay with *not* always understanding the situation we're in. This is why Buddhism is often referred to as the Path of Liberation. Liberation is the moment you don't react to being cut off in traffic—because you don't know what actually happened, so there's nothing to react *to*. Liberation is experiencing reality as it is.

What does the word *Buddha* mean?

Buddha is a word that means "awakened one" or "a person who is awake" in both Sanskrit and Pali. The idea of awakening and being awake runs throughout Buddhist philosophy. Buddhism teaches that there's reality as it is, and then there's reality as we humans perceive or understand it. Our perception of reality is influenced by how our minds are conditioned; in other words, our ideas, cultural beliefs, concepts, and opinions all directly affect how we see reality. A Buddha is someone who is completely liberated from the mistaken perceptions of reality to which we are all so susceptible, thus experiencing *nirvana* (a Sanskrit word meaning "blown out" or "extinguished"), which is the state of awakened understanding of existence that is the ultimate goal of Buddhist practice.

What did the Buddha do after he became enlightened?

After his enlightenment, the Buddha dedicated the rest of his life to teaching others how to realize enlightenment for themselves. He gave his first sermon to the other mendicant monks with whom he'd been living during his time of intense physical practice. They joined him, and together they traveled from village to village, spreading his teachings and eventually founding the original order of Buddhist nuns and monks. The Buddha died at about 80 years old, but his teachings continue to spread around the world today.

Did the Buddha have a family?

Before becoming the Buddha, Siddhartha Gautama
married a woman named Yasodhara, and they had a
son named Rahula. Yasodhara and Rahula remained in
the palace during the years Siddhartha was seeking his
enlightenment, but tradition says they joined the order of
monks and nuns he later established. The Buddha didn't
have any siblings, but several of his cousins also joined his
order and became monks. His cousin Ananda is the monk
who memorized his teachings and sermons, which would
be spread orally until the Pali Canon was written. The
Buddha's family, friends, and disciples were instrumental
in spreading his teachings far and wide.

I've seen statues and paintings of a fat, happy Buddha. Is that what the Buddha looked like?

Because *Buddha* is a title meaning "awakened one," there have been many Buddhas throughout history. One such person was a Chinese Buddhist monk called Budai, also known as the Laughing Buddha or the Fat Buddha. When you see a statue of a fat, bald man with a smile, you're seeing Budai, not Siddhartha Gautama, on whose teachings Buddhism was founded. To distinguish Siddhartha from other Buddhas, Buddhists often refer to him as either Gautama Buddha or Shakyamuni Buddha ("sage of the Shakyas," the Shakyas being his clan). Most depictions of Gautama Buddha show a thin man with long ears, usually in the pose of sitting meditation.

Do Buddhists consider the Buddha to be a god? Do Buddhists worship the Buddha?

The Buddha was a teacher, not a god. When you see Buddhists bowing to statues or images of the Buddha, they're not necessarily worshipping him but rather making a physical expression of their humble intent to follow the Buddha's teachings in order to overcome an ego-centered life. In fact, in one Buddhist scripture, the Buddha seems to be critical of god worship, telling a young man that it's far more important to live ethically than it is to worship anything. Over time, though, the various schools of Buddhism have come to view the Buddha in different ways; some almost seem to deify and worship him, while others simply hold him in the highest esteem and treat him as the ultimate teacher. While there is no doctrine about the Buddha being anything other than a man and a teacher, there are certainly cultural practices in some Buddhist traditions in which the Buddha is described as a type of god, though not a creator God like we think of in Judeo-Christian and Islamic traditions.

*Should you find a wise critic
to point out your faults,
follow him as you would
a guide to hidden treasure.*

**THE BUDDHA,
THE DHAMMAPADA**

So if his main role was being a teacher, what exactly did the Buddha teach?

When the Buddha achieved enlightenment, he realized that in order to really understand enlightenment, a person has to experience certain aspects of it directly. No words or concepts can adequately express what enlightenment *is*.

This means that enlightenment can't be explained; it has to be experienced. So instead of teaching a set of beliefs, the Buddha taught a set of practices, a method to help people realize enlightenment for themselves. The Buddha's teachings are meant to be put into practice, and the resulting experiences are to be verified by each individual practitioner. Instead of determining whether these teachings are *true* or not, we are encouraged to verify if they *work* or not. In other words, do these teachings really lead to the reduction, and ultimately the cessation, of suffering?

The aim of Buddhism is to help us understand the nature of reality and suffering and let go of the causes of suffering. This process starts with taking a critical look at how we see the world. Thich Nhat Hanh, a Zen Buddhist monk, says that "the secret of Buddhism is to remove all ideas, all concepts, in order for the truth to have a chance to penetrate, to reveal itself."

The Buddha taught that we are essentially prisoners of our own minds, bound by our beliefs, perceptions, and ideas. We see an inaccurate version of reality—a version, not coincidentally, that causes us unnecessary suffering.

We tend to go through life thinking that external circumstances are to blame for our suffering and our lack of contentment. The Buddha's teachings help us alter that perspective and learn that the unnecessary suffering we experience has more to do with *how* we see things than with *what* we see. It's an internal change, not an external one, that will bring about the joy and contentment we seek. The core of the Buddha's teachings will be discussed in more detail in part 3 of this book.

Chris Wasn't There

A few years ago, I had to bring on a new supplier for a special product my photography-gear company was working on. I connected with Chris, the head of sales at the new supplier's factory, to work on prototyping the product virtually. After several months of e-mailing back and forth, we needed to meet in person. But when I got to the meeting place, I didn't see Chris anywhere.

I checked my e-mail and confirmed that I was in the right place at the right time. Maybe Chris was running late. I waited a few minutes. No Chris. I waited a few more minutes. Still no Chris. By now I was pacing back and forth, impatiently wondering, "Where is he?" Finally, I sat down on a nearby bench, where two young women were also sitting, and pulled out my phone to call Chris and ask what was taking him so long. Before I could do that, one of the women turned around and said, "Hi, are you Noah? I'm Chris!" I started laughing, and when I told her why I was laughing, she laughed, too.

Aside from being funny, this story exemplifies how beliefs can affect our understanding of reality. I believed that Chris was a man, so I thought he was kind of a jerk for being late. It never occurred to me that Chris might be right where she was supposed to be, because I thought she was a he! My inaccurate belief blinded me to the reality of the situation. How many realities are we blind to simply because we already hold an idea, concept, or belief that prevents us from seeing reality as it is?

When did the Buddha die? Did another spiritual leader take his place?

The Buddha died around the age of 80 from a sudden illness, possibly food poisoning, after eating a meal offered by a lay follower. He did not name a successor. Ananda, the Buddha's cousin and attendant, had asked him before his death, "Who will teach us when you are gone?" The Buddha advised him that his teachings would serve as the teacher. Today, there are representatives of many schools of Buddhism around the world who continue to spread his teachings. Even if you don't have much experience with Buddhism, you've probably heard of some of these, like Tenzin Gyatso, better known as the Dalai Lama, of the Tibetan Buddhist tradition. It's important, however, to know that an individual teacher in one school or tradition does not represent Buddhism as a whole and may not always agree with teachers in other traditions.

I've heard people say that Buddhism is more a way of life than a religion. Did the Buddha teach a way of life, a religion, or a philosophy?

Perhaps the best answer is "all of the above." If you search any list of major world religions, you'll certainly find Buddhism on that list, but Buddhism is different from most religions in that it's a nontheistic tradition; it doesn't espouse a belief in a supreme creator God as the source of existence. Furthermore, Buddhism isn't concerned with many of the big questions asked by other religions, like: Is there a God? What happens when we die? Is the universe finite or infinite?

In the Buddhist parable of the poisoned arrow, a monk is so troubled that the Buddha hasn't addressed these types of existential questions that he threatens to abandon his monastic vows unless he can get satisfactory answers. The Buddha responds by comparing him to a man wounded with a poisoned arrow who, absurdly, won't accept treatment until he knows who shot him, what clan the archer was from, what the archer looked like, what materials the arrow was made of, and so on. "The man would die," the Buddha concludes, "and those things would still remain unknown to him" (Majjhima Nikāya 63).

This story nicely illustrates how Buddhism takes a pragmatic approach to tackling the challenge immediately at hand: that in life, difficulties arise and we experience suffering, much as we would if shot by a poison arrow. The Buddha taught that the wise thing to do is not to spend time and energy focusing on irrelevant details but to remove the arrow. Rather than trying to answer these existential questions, Buddhism urges us to look inward and ask ourselves, "Why do I feel the need to know these things?"

Because Buddhism is less concerned with big, unknowable, supernatural questions, we can comfortably say that Buddhism, in addition to being a religion, is a way of life or a philosophy: a set of practices that don't depend on any dogmatic beliefs, a way to live that maximizes our chances for peace and contentment in the present moment—which is, after all, the only moment we'll ever have. The Buddha encouraged his followers to test his teachings for themselves in their own lives. As you read through the rest of this book, I encourage you to examine these teachings, put them into practice, and determine for yourself if they are relevant to you.

Is there a Buddhist Bible or other authoritative text that all Buddhists use?

The short answer is no. Various schools of Buddhism use different texts and writings as the source of their teachings, and a text that's venerated in one school may be completely unknown in another. For example, the oldest collection of Buddhist writings, the Tipiṭaka (known in English as the Pali Canon) is the standard collection of scriptures for Theravada Buddhists. *Tipiṭaka* is Pali for "three baskets," and the text is split into three general categories: the Vinaya Piṭaka (the "discipline basket," which contains rules of discipline for followers), the Sutta Piṭaka (the "sayings basket," which contains the discourses and sermons of the Buddha), and the Abhidhamma Piṭaka (the "higher teaching basket," which contains Buddhist doctrines about the mind). The Vinaya Piṭaka and Sutta Piṭaka contain very similar teachings to the texts and works of other early Buddhist schools, while the Abhidhamma Piṭaka is a Theravada collection that doesn't have much in common with scriptures recognized by other denominations.

Other writings are used in other schools of Buddhism. In the Mahayana schools, including Zen, some of the most popular scriptures are the *Heart Sutra*, the *Lotus Sutra,* and the *Diamond Sutra*. Another popular Buddhist text is the Dhammapada, a collection of sayings of the Buddha.

It's important to know that Buddhist texts are not equivalent to writings like the Bible in other spiritual traditions. Buddhist writings are not considered to be dictated or revealed by a deity. They're meant to guide us on the path of enlightenment, not to indoctrinate us in a particular set of beliefs. Buddhist teachings are not something you're meant to *believe*; they're something you *do*—you put them into practice.

You've mentioned various "schools" of Buddhism. What are the major types of Buddhism?

The Buddha's teachings began to spread out of India and Nepal into neighboring countries in Asia and have continued to spread for 2,500 years. In that time, Buddhism has divided into several sects or schools, each with its own practices, rituals, and writings. While all the schools are founded on the same basic teachings, there are some differences.

The two major branches of Buddhism are Theravada and Mahayana. Mahayana has several subsets that you may have heard of, like Zen, Tibetan, and Pure Land Buddhism. There is also an extension of Mahayana Buddhism called Vajrayana, which is sometimes referred to as a distinct, third branch of Buddhism.

Theravada is the main form of Buddhism in Sri Lanka, Thailand, Cambodia, Myanmar, and Laos, while Mahayana dominates in China, Japan, Taiwan, Nepal, Mongolia, Korea, and Vietnam. Vajrayana is the main form of Buddhism practiced in Tibet and the form that the Dalai Lama practices and teaches. Of the various forms of Buddhism that exist today, Theravada is the oldest, but Mahayana has the most practitioners. Many denominations of Buddhism, like Zen, Tibetan, Jōdo Shinshū, and Nichiren, may seem quite different on the surface, but all forms of Buddhism are built on the same general foundation and share many of the same core concepts and teachings.

The Evolution of Ideas

Growing up, I spent several years living in Mexico, speaking both English and Spanish in my home. I remember feeling concerned about my accent: The American accents on TV were different from the ones I heard growing up in Texas, while the people in Mexico City spoke Spanish with a different accent than I did. I wanted to be sure I had the "right" accent. Similarly, when I first started studying Buddhism, I wanted to study the "right" kind. Was that Theravada? Zen? Something else entirely?

But ideas, like languages, change over time. People have developed different American accents in different regions of the United States, and the Spanish spoken in Mexico is different from the Spanish spoken in other Latin American countries and in Spain. Likewise, Buddhism has evolved to fit different cultures and time periods. There's no right or wrong form of Buddhism to practice, just like there's no right or wrong accent in which to speak English or Spanish. The Buddha said that the greatest of all teachings is the teaching of impermanence. How could Buddhism possibly stay the same in a world that's constantly changing? You can learn something from all the various Buddhist traditions, finding which teachings ring true for you and resonate with your specific personality or learning style. And as you change, your practice can change with you.

What are the main differences between Theravada, Mahayana, and Vajrayana Buddhism?

Though it's difficult to make any blanket statements that would hold true for all sects within a given school, in general, the two main schools of Buddhism differ primarily in what they consider the ultimate goal of their practice. In Theravada Buddhism, it's to become an *arhat*, a practitioner who follows the Buddha's path and realizes enlightenment. In Mahayana Buddhism, the goal is to become a *bodhisattva*, one who vows not only to become awakened but also to awaken all other beings. This difference in approaches arises from the Mahayana view of interdependence, which holds that one being can't be fully enlightened unless and until all beings are enlightened. Vajrayana Buddhism, an off-shoot of Mahayana, also focuses on the bodhisattva vow and adds various forms of intensive meditation practice to help practitioners directly connect to the awakened Buddha-nature within. (The concept of Buddha-nature will be discussed more in part 2.)

Another key difference is that Theravada Buddhism is primarily a monastic practice, meaning that most prac-titioners have renounced their ordinary lives and taken vows to become full-time monks or nuns. The lay commu-nity provides support for the monastic community, but laypeople don't necessarily follow the same devotional path to enlightenment. In Mahayana schools, it's more common to find a devotional path for laypeople who aren't interested in becoming monks or nuns. For example, a Zen priest may be married and have an ordinary full-time job while also spending time on contemplative practices.

The various traditions also rely on different texts for their teachings. Theravada Buddhism follows the Pali Canon exclusively, while Mahayana practice is based on the Tibetan and Chinese Buddhist canons. The Tibetan and Chinese canons contain some texts that correspond to the early Pali Canon but also include several that are strictly Mahayana, which Theravada Buddhists don't consider legitimate. Because the different canons are in different languages, Theravada schools tend to use the Pali form of common terms, like *sutta* and *dhamma*, while Mahayana uses the Sanskrit versions (*sutra, dharma*).

Additionally, some schools, like Zen, may emphasize meditation as the key to practice, while others will augment meditation by chanting a mantra, and still others won't place much importance on meditation at all.

I hear the word *Zen* used a lot when people talk about Buddhism. What is Zen?

Zen is a form of Mahayana Buddhism that originated in China around the sixth century CE, then spread to Japan and beyond. It's notable for its focus on meditation, including extensive *zazen*, or "seated meditation." Many of the teachers who popularized Buddhism in the West were from this school, which is why some Westerners think of Zen as being synonymous with Buddhism or even use the word *Zen* to mean "calm," "relaxed," or "being in the moment."

How did Buddhism come to the West?

Buddhism began to arrive in the United States through Chinese immigrants in the mid-1800s, as well as through Americans and Europeans who had visited Asia and brought Buddhist texts and ideas back with them. Buddhist concepts began showing up in the literary works of authors like Walt Whitman, Henry David Thoreau, and Ralph Waldo Emerson. In the late 1800s, several Japanese forms of Buddhism, including Pure Land and Zen, were beginning to take form in the United States, and by the 1950s and '60s, there were Zen centers established in both Los Angeles and San Francisco. Spiritual seekers, like Joseph Goldstein, Jack Kornfield, Sharon Salzberg, Jon Kabat-Zinn, and many others, became interested in Buddhism and Eastern philosophy and began pioneering new ways to use meditation as a tool for health care and stress reduction.

More recently, Buddhism has gained popularity as celebrities and artists like Leonard Cohen, Richard Gere, Herbie Hancock, Phil Jackson, and Tina Turner have openly shared the influence that Buddhism has had on their lives and work. Today, Buddhism in the West is no longer niche. There are thousands of Americans and Europeans who were raised Buddhist, have converted to Buddhism, or practice Buddhism as a philosophy of life.

PART 2
CORE CONCEPTS

What You'll Learn: In this section, you'll learn about some of the key concepts that run throughout Buddhist ideas and teachings, such as suffering, impermanence, and enlightenment. Understanding the ideas at the core of Buddhism will give you deeper insight into how we can best use them to live peacefully and with compassion for all. Understanding these basic concepts will help you as you explore Buddhism through this book and beyond.

The Buddha became a great teacher after he became enlightened. But what is enlightenment? Can anyone become enlightened?

Enlightenment is the ultimate goal of all Buddhist teachings and practices, and the Buddha taught that anyone—that means you!—can realize enlightenment. That's what Buddhist teachings and practices are for— to help regular people like you and me along the path to that goal. The Buddhist conception of enlightenment isn't intellectual. It's experiential. It's kind of like being a parent: If I went back in time and tried to explain to my younger self what it feels like to be a dad, nothing I could say would adequately convey it. I couldn't imagine what it would feel like to be a dad until I actually became one. In the same way, you cannot truly know what it's like to be enlightened unless you've realized enlightenment. Having said that, there are some ways to describe enlightenment that point us in the direction of what the experience is like. The Buddha said that "just as the great ocean has one taste, the taste of salt, so also this teaching and discipline has one taste, the taste of liberation" (Udāna 5.5). To be enlightened is to be liberated from our habitual reactivity, freed from our perceptions and ideas in order to see reality as it is without wanting it to be different.

I would go further and say that enlightenment is also freedom from wanting to be enlightened. Any notion we have about what enlightenment is can get in the way of actually experiencing it. Put another way, enlightenment isn't something you get or find; it's something you rediscover—a state of being that has always been in you but that has been covered with made-up stories and false concepts. Buddhism teaches that enlightenment is our true nature. It's not something we can become, because it's something we already are. We just have to realize it.

What about the word *awakening*? Is it different from *enlightenment*?

Some people, including some Buddhists, use both words to refer to essentially the same thing, but I see them as being slightly different. I think of enlightenment as the experience and understanding of reality just as it is, without the influence of the concepts, ideas, and beliefs that so often muddy our perception of it. Awakening, on the other hand, is the process by which this new way of seeing life begins to unfold. I see awakening as a path with several stages and levels, while the final, radical shift in perspective is the moment of enlightenment.

This idea is conveyed by a famous koan (a paradoxical statement that Zen Buddhists meditate on) that says you can enter this state of awakening only through a gateless gate. This is a seemingly simple but rather profound teaching: As long as you think there is a gate, you will not be able to enter the awakened state. You enter it by realizing there is no gate; you've been in that awakened state all along. You arrive there by realizing there is no "there" there. The only thing keeping you from seeing this is the mistaken belief that you were ever outside a gate in the first place. In a way, you become awakened the moment you realize you don't need to *become* awakened—everything you need to know is already present within you.

What does Buddhism teach about good and evil?

From the Buddhist perspective, good and evil are not inherent forces out in the universe; instead, they're internal states of mind. Buddhism teaches us to look inward. There we can find the source of all the good things we say, think, and do, and likewise discover that we ourselves—our own minds—are the source of any evil. This understanding gives us a greater sense of responsibility over our own thoughts, words, and actions.

Rather than thinking of evil as an external agent acting upon us, Buddhism teaches that greed, hatred, and ignorance are the sources of what we typically think of as "evil." In Buddhism, these three qualities are called "the three poisons" or "the three fires." The challenge the three poisons pose in our lives is that they drive us to look outside of ourselves to try to achieve happiness or avoid suffering. Because external things, like money, fame, or power, can't bring us lasting joy or contentment, we're setting ourselves up to experience unnecessary suffering by chasing after them. Material things can be nice to have for a time, but the happiness and fulfillment we seek is not found in external sources.

Why does Buddhism consider ignorance to be a poison? What's wrong with not knowing things?

From the Buddhist perspective, calling ignorance a poison is specifically referring to a lack of understanding about the nature of reality. So, for example, when we perceive things to be permanent and independent from other things, this blinds us from seeing things as they truly are: impermanent and interdependent. This misconception fuels our suffering.

The most dangerous manifestation of ignorance is the belief in a permanent self that exists independent of other people and the rest of the world. Clinging to this false, or ignorant, sense of self and wanting to protect it give rise to greed and hatred. Ignorance is a poison because it prevents us from seeing things as they are, which is necessary to reach enlightenment. The antidote to ignorance is wisdom about the nature of both reality and the self.

As a water bead
on a lotus leaf,
as water on a red lily,
does not adhere,
so the sage
does not adhere
to the seen,
the heard,
or the sensed.

THE BUDDHA,
THE SUTTA NIPATA

Why is greed considered to be a poison? Is it wrong to desire things like good food or a nice car?

Greed is the mental state we experience when we want to get more of what we want, whenever possible, at whatever cost to others. It's one of the three poisons because of the effect is has on our minds. We often believe the misguided notion that if we could just get the things we want—money, fame, power—they would somehow finally give us the happiness we seek and ensure we'd no longer experience suffering. Greed is not just about material things, though. We also tend to want to change other people to get more things, like attention or affection. We mistakenly think that once we change others, we'll find lasting happiness.

A skillful way of dealing with the poison of greed is to try to understand it. We start that process by looking at the things we desire and asking ourselves, "Why?" Why do I feel such a strong desire to have this thing or that person? Why do I feel the need to achieve this or that? It's not that there's anything inherently wrong with the feeling of desire; it's that we can become blinded by it, especially when we don't have a thorough understanding of the intent or causes behind why we feel what we feel. Simply following our desires without taking time to understand them can lead to destructive behavior and mental confusion, which is why greed is considered a poison.

Why is hatred considered to be a poison? Is it wrong to ever feel hate?

Hatred is what we feel when we want to harm anyone or anything that stands in the way of getting what we want—anyone or anything that poses, or seems to pose, some kind of threat to us. Buddhism teaches that hatred is a poison because it can so easily consume all our time and energy. It can't just be removed from us; in order to be free from the bonds of hatred, we have to practice a different way of perceiving what happens to us.

From the Buddhist perspective, letting go of hatred is not a moral issue. The problem with hatred isn't whether it's morally right or wrong. Clinging to hatred is simply an unwise action because it creates unnecessary suffering for ourselves and others. As a mental state, hatred affects the emotional well-being of the person doing the hating more than the person being hated. So it's not *wrong* to feel hatred; in fact, it's natural to feel this emotion from time to time. It is, however, wise to try to understand why we feel it. What other emotions might be hidden underneath the hatred? Are feelings of sadness, loneliness, or vulnerability in some way causing the emotion of hatred to arise? Rather than evading the painful truth of how we feel, Buddhism encourages us to embrace the reality of our feelings, including any feelings of hatred we might be experiencing. We strive to understand the causes and conditions that allow the feeling of hatred to arise, turning inward for understanding rather than acting on destructive impulses.

Making Moments of Awareness

What are moments of awareness, and how can you create them? Let me describe an example from my own life. I sometimes work as a substitute school-bus driver. There's a window of about 15 minutes between the time I drop off the high school students and the time I need to head back out to start picking up the elementary school students. I usually use that time to practice meditation.

One morning, during that window, I started my practice by asking myself two questions: "Where am I?" and "What am I doing?" These questions may seem simple, but it can be tricky to focus on them. It seems like no matter where we are or what we're doing, we're always thinking of somewhere or something else. Those two questions often help me think deeply about where I am, anchoring me to the present moment.

In this instance, I was sitting on the school bus. There were many other places I could be, but that happened to be where I was. Once I was feeling present in the moment, I asked myself a third question: "What did it take for this moment to arise?" In my mind, I began exploring the possible people and processes that had allowed the moment to exist just the way it was. I looked at the radio that I use to communicate with the school and the other bus drivers. I looked at the mirror, thinking about the materials and labor that went into it. I looked at the rivets in the ceiling of the bus and the different panels and buttons, and I thought about how they all connected. This process went on and on, stretching across moments. I started to think about everything taking place across town just before I headed out to start picking up students. Kids were waking up—that required alarm clocks or smartphones. Parents were drinking coffee—where did that coffee come from? I was thinking about coffee farmers and their crops when suddenly I noticed how all these incredibly complex processes that had been in motion for a very long time were now about to culminate with my driving up to a child's house and opening the school-bus door so the child could climb on.

I think of moments like these as moments of awareness. From a Buddhist perspective, these moments allow us to make contact, even if only briefly, with reality as it is, as opposed to the stories and chatter in our heads that we're usually tuned into. Not only that, but moments of awareness evoke a tremendous sense of gratitude and awe, and they can be experienced anywhere at any time. You can try this yourself by asking, "Where am I? What am I doing? What did it take for this moment to arise?"

Some religions teach that people are inherently bad and that they must overcome that badness by following a specific set of beliefs or practices. From the Buddhist perspective, are people inherently good or bad?

From the Buddhist perspective, people are neither inherently good nor inherently bad, but we all have the potential to connect with an inner kindness and compassion known as Buddha-nature. The main idea here is that we're hardwired as social creatures to be kind and loving to each other. From the moment we're born, we depend entirely on the kindness and compassion of others, like the parents or caretakers who keep us alive. But over time, our minds become conditioned by beliefs and concepts that we acquire from our families and society. We learn about concepts like self and other, us and them, right and wrong, good and bad—concepts that divide our perception of the world and ourselves into separate categories. Such dichotomizing concepts can cover up our Buddha-nature, that inborn state of kindness, compassion, and interconnectedness with others and the world.

There's a story about a monastery in Thailand where the resident monks covered a golden statue of the Buddha in clay to hide its value from an invading army. Those monks were killed during the invasion. Over the course of many years, a new group of monks moved in, and the golden Buddha remained hidden under a layer of clay. One day, the new monks decided it was time to relocate the old clay statue of the Buddha, and in the process of moving it, a piece of clay broke off to reveal the brilliant golden Buddha underneath.

This story symbolizes how Buddhists view the natural state of awareness, kindness, and compassion in us all. To see this inherent nature in ourselves and others, we have to peel away the clay—all the ideas, opinions, and beliefs that are preventing us from seeing how things really are.

What is truth, from the Buddhist perspective? Is anything absolutely true or absolutely false in this worldview?

Buddhism teaches that there are truths that are true whether we believe them or not, and then there are truths that are true simply because we believe they are true. For example, when the temperature outside drops below 32 degrees Fahrenheit and there is sufficient moisture in the air, it will snow instead of rain. This is true whether we believe it or not. On the other hand, it is true that gold is more valuable than silver only because we collectively believe it to be so. If there were no humans on the planet, gold and silver would have no inherent value. It's a conceptual truth.

We live in a world full of conceptual truths, but it's easy to forget that. Our incredibly complex social, political, financial, and religious systems all depend on shared, agreed-upon beliefs. We wouldn't be able to trade paper money for goods, like bread and milk, unless we collectively believed that a piece of paper or metal had real value. But the value of a five-dollar bill is not true in the same way the existence of snow is true.

This Buddhist understanding of truth is encapsulated in the parable of the six blind men who stand around an elephant and begin to describe it on the basis of what they can feel by touch. One feels the tail and thinks he's touching a rope, while another feels the trunk and concludes it's a snake. The other men describe what they touch as a tree trunk (the elephant's leg), a fan (its ear), a wall (its side), and a spear (its tusk). Each man is certain that his experience of the elephant is the accurate one, failing to understand that the other descriptions are also accurate—and that all the descriptions are inaccurate as well, in that they each take into account only one part of the elephant. Buddhism teaches that we all see the truth from a unique perspective and that, like the blind men, we can't see all perspectives. We're bound by space and time to one unique view in the here and now.

There are also, however, some absolute or universal truths taught in Buddhism, and these are not bound by space and time or constructed by collective agreement. The Buddha taught that there are three universal characteristics of life, also known as the three marks of existence: *dukkha* (suffering), *anicca* (impermanence), and *anattā* (nonself). These three concepts form the core of what could be considered the truth in Buddhism.

When Buddhists say everything is impermanent, what do they mean?

The Buddha taught that, along with suffering and non-self, impermanence—or *anicca*—is one of the three marks of existence in life. The nature of reality is that all things are constantly changing, and therefore all things are impermanent. Jobs, relationships, good times, bad times, our thoughts and feelings, our loved ones, our own selves—literally everything we know of or perceive— will pass out of existence. The problem is that even if we know this, we continue to cling to things as if they were permanent because we want them to last. When we look at the world around us—city streets and buildings, trees and lakes—we perceive it to be solid and fixed. We know intellectually that one day those trees will die and those buildings will crumble, but we continue to *perceive* them as permanent.

Buddhism teaches two types of impermanence: gross and subtle. Gross impermanence happens on a larger scale: Matter decays, people die, empires rise and fall, societal norms change and evolve. This is the kind of impermanence we see all around us. Like clouds, things arise, endure for a while, and then pass. Subtle impermanence, meanwhile, is smaller-scale, moment-to-moment change. At this very instant, you are physically undergoing change as the cells in your body die and regenerate. You are not the same exact person from moment to moment. Instead of seeing ourselves as fixed, semipermanent entities, we can start to see ourselves as we truly are: collections of impermanent, momentary experiences.

When we start to understand the nature of impermanence, our tendency to cling to outcomes and expectations will begin to diminish. That doesn't mean it's suddenly easy to lose a job or a loved one. It just means that the suffering of loss will go more smoothly when we learn to see things as they really are: that loss is a natural part of the course of life, rather than something we need to fight against. When we understand that all things are impermanent, we can begin to find meaning and joy in every moment as it passes.

I've heard that Buddhists think life is suffering. Does that mean they think life is all bad? What do they mean by the word *suffering*?

Buddhists believe that suffering is an inherent part of life—so inherent that it's classified as one of the three marks of existence. But that doesn't mean Buddhists believe life is all bad. The Pali word for "suffering," *dukkha*, has also been rendered as "unsatisfactoriness" and "anguish." It's a concept that seems to be difficult to translate into a single English word, but it's essential to understand as so much of Buddhist philosophy is built around it.

Buddhism teaches that there are three different types of suffering. The first is called "the suffering of suffering." This is a natural form of suffering that we experience on a regular basis. *Pain* might be a good word to summarize it. It's what we experience when we stub our toe, stay up all night with the stomach flu, or start to feel achy as we age.

The second type of suffering is called "the suffering of loss." This is what we experience when, for example, we lose a job, a loved one, or our youth and vitality. This form of suffering is also natural, and like the suffering of suffering, it's often connected to specific circumstances.

The third type of suffering is called "the all-pervasive suffering," and it's the type Buddhism is most concerned with. Unlike the first two types, all-pervasive suffering is self-inflicted, and it generally arises out of an ignorant or delusional understanding of reality. It tends to have very little to do with our actual circumstances and a lot to do with how we *perceive* and *interpret* those circumstances.

Our beliefs around body image are a good example. Our culture's subjective notion of an ideal body is reinforced by advertisements, television, and movies, with the result that society as a whole begins to collectively believe that there is indeed an ideal body or look. In reality, that idealized type is something we simply made up. But because most of us live unaware of the constructed nature of this apparent "truth," people end up feeling discomfort or suffering about how they look when they perceive they've fallen short of the ideal.

That kind of suffering is self-inflicted, based on a belief or concept, not on circumstances themselves. If we didn't hold the false belief, the suffering wouldn't exist. This all-pervasive suffering is difficult for us to detect because it requires us to scrutinize our deeply held views, ideas, and beliefs. But when we are able to do that, we gain insight and wisdom into the nature of our own self-inflicted suffering. That's the first step in releasing its hold on us.

What does the Buddhist concept of nonself mean? Obviously I have a self—my self is sitting here reading about Buddhism! Do Buddhists think I don't exist?

The third mark of existence, along with suffering and impermanence, is *anattā*, which translates to "nonself" or "no-self." This teaching doesn't imply that you don't exist; rather, it means that you're not what you think you are because there is no inherent essence in anything. In other words, things *are* because of, and in relation to, other things, but things do not exist by themselves as permanent or separate entities. Everything is inter-dependent. The main idea behind this concept is that we tend to see things—including, or perhaps especially, ourselves—as individual beings. I perceive myself as separate from others and others as separate from me. The irony is that we each exist in the most fundamental sense only because of the actions of other people, namely, our parents. Without any effort on your part, certain causes and conditions resulted in your existence here and now. This is true of all things. Everything has causes and conditions; nothing stands alone.

I went to helicopter flight school for a couple of years after college, so I can tell you firsthand that when you're piloting a helicopter, you have to continually use all four limbs to work the various buttons, bars, levers, and throttles that control the speed, direction, and elevation of the helicopter. You don't just lock these things into place and relax. You're constantly adjusting everything in order to stay in the air. The Buddhist teaching of nonself sees living things in much the same way. We're always making adjustments as we go, so there's no fixed, permanent version of us, only the continually changing combination of causes and conditions. Are you more you when you're hungry or when you've recently eaten a meal? Is the authentic you the one that's well rested or the one who's sleep-deprived because you've been laboring over a work project for the past week? Is the real you the one who was raised in a loving home or the one who endured an experience of trauma as a child? The Buddhist teaching of nonself says that there is no permanent or fixed you—there's only a complex web of inseparable, impermanent causes and effects.

Which Me Is Really Me?

When you look at a car, you might see just a car, an independent object separate from everything around it. But in reality, the car is dependent on all the parts and processes that allow it to exist. If you were to disassemble it into all its parts and spread them out in the parking lot, you couldn't point to which one of those parts was the car. No one single part of the car—engine, tire, or rearview mirror—*is* the car. A car is the sum of all its parts.

Try this yourself. You can take anything and break it down to its parts—literally if it's something like a pen, mentally if it's something like a car. You'll see very quickly how all things are dependent on causes and conditions, the parts that allow a thing to be what it is. When we understand this, we experience a major shift in how we see the world. We start to see ourselves as dependent on everything that makes us who we are. We are the sum total of all our parts (and we ourselves are parts of families, communities, societies).

Ask yourself, "Which me is the real me?" This question helps me remember that there is no permanent me. There is only the momentary me that is continually changing and being changed by everything around me. The me of now is not the me of yesterday or five years ago or five years from now. This is what Buddhism teaches with regard to nonself.

*"All experiences are
preceded by mind,
having mind
as their master,
created by mind."*

**THE BUDDHA,
THE DHAMMAPADA**

What is nonattachment, and why is it important in Buddhism? Does it mean I'm not supposed be attached to things that are important to me, like family?

One of the most frequent misconceptions I hear about Buddhism is that it teaches that we must become *detached* from things: possessions, people, expectations, and so on. That's not really what those teachings are about. What Buddhism does teach is a concept called nonattachment, which is different from detachment.

To understand nonattachment more clearly, we must first understand that in order to be attached, two things are required: the person who is attached and the object of the attachment. But, as we just learned above, there is no "self" that's doing the attaching. Buddhism teaches that it's our ignorant view of a separate self that causes us to cling to "other" things: people, relationships, material objects. In other words, attachment is what we experience when we're living inside the illusion of a permanent, separate self. Nonattachment occurs when we have realized the truth of nonself.

Think about attachment in the context of the labels we apply to ourselves: our job titles, belief systems, political views, opinions, and so on. We attach to these concepts and identify with them to the point that we feel tremendous suffering when they're attacked or we lose them. Our tendency is to think that we must be either attached strongly to an idea or detached from that idea entirely.

Buddhism proposes a different option: We can be non-attached to our ideas. Without dropping our labels and concepts completely, we loosen the death grip we have on them. When someone attacks a belief or opinion we hold, we can see that they're attacking the idea, not us directly. When we're nonattached to our ideas, they no longer own us—we own them.

What do Buddhists mean when they talk about emptiness? Are they saying life is meaningless and empty?

The Buddhist understanding of emptiness is that all things are devoid of meaning until we assign meaning to them. Reality is like a blank canvas, bare until the painter comes along and creates something on that emptiness.

Words are a good example of something naturally empty that we nonetheless experience as full of meaning. Every word you know is simply a combination of sounds, completely devoid of meaning until someone at some point in history decided that its particular sound should have a particular meaning. If we didn't assign meaning to the sounds we make, they would just be sounds. From the Buddhist perspective, all things are like this: empty of inherent meaning. That's not to say they're meaningless. It's just that the meaning comes from us, the givers of meaning, not from the things themselves. There's what is, and then there's the story we create about it.

There's a wonderful Buddhist parable that illustrates this concept well: One day, an old farmer is out working in the field when, out of the blue, a horse appears. The farmer's neighbor comes running over and exclaims, "How fortunate you are! A horse has appeared out of nowhere, and now it's yours!"

The farmer simply replies, "Who knows what is good and what is bad?"

The following day, the farmer discovers that the horse has broken out of the corral and run away. The neighbor comes running over and exclaims, "How unfortunate for you! Your horse is now gone!"

The farmer simply replies, "Who knows what is good and what is bad?"

Later that day, the horse shows up back in the field with four additional horses. Once again, the neighbor interprets this as good fortune, and once again, the farmer replies, "Who knows what is good and what is bad?"

Later, the farmer's son falls off one of the horses while riding and breaks his leg. "How unfortunate," says the neighbor. "Your only son has a broken leg!"

But the farmer simply replies, "Who knows what is good and what is bad?"

The next day, the army comes to town to conscript all the young men for a war, but it can't take the farmer's son because of his broken leg. The neighbor comes running over and says, "How fortunate for you. My son was taken, but yours has a broken leg and because of that . . ."

He pauses and simply says, together with the farmer, "Who knows what is good and what is bad?"

This is emptiness. It's the understanding that as life unfolds, it doesn't mean anything. It is neither positive nor negative. All things simply are as they are.

What is the Buddhist understanding of death? Is there an afterlife in Buddhism?

If you recall the parable of the poisoned arrow from part 1, you'll remember that the Buddha never answered many of the existential questions we so often want to know about. From the Buddhist perspective, birth and death are not the beginning and end; they are not separate from one another. Death is simply the culmination of a phase that started with birth, but the overall process of life started long before our individual births and deaths, and it will continue long after.

Life is a lot like music, and our lives are like songs. While songs all have a starting note and an ending note, even when a song ends, music itself goes on, regardless of what song is playing. And the beauty of each song is found in the continual changing of the notes, including the eventual final note that marks the end of the song.

Death represents the end of what is familiar, and we're often uncomfortable with or scared of the unknown music that's beyond the final note in the song of our own lives. But in reality, there's no need to fear death, because while it may be the end of the song, it's not the end of music.

An understanding of impermanence and interdependence can ease the fear of death by reminding us that birth wasn't the start and death won't be the end. Every beginning has an end, and every end gives birth to a new beginning. There really is no beginning or end; there is only change.

So rather than focusing on life after death, we can instead choose to focus on life before death—the life we're living now. Rather than speculating about what happens when we die, we can anchor ourselves in the present moment.

Do Buddhists believe in reincarnation?

Buddhists believe in rebirth, which is not quite the same thing as what you probably have in mind when you think about reincarnation. The traditional conception of reincarnation is that you—some kind of soul or spirit—go on to inhabit a new physical form, whether it be a person, animal, or plant. Though some Buddhist schools think of rebirth as something closer to this idea of reincarnation, it doesn't fit with other Buddhists' understanding of impermanence and nonself. We're changing form every day, experiencing rebirth even from one moment to the next. The you that's reading this page is literally not the same you who will be reading the last page of the book. If there is no permanent you, what part of you could transcend death to become reincarnated?

Yet when we observe nature, we see constant rebirth. After all, the law of conservation of energy in physics states that energy can't be created or destroyed; it can just be transformed from one form into another. A cloud changes form and becomes rain. The rain becomes part of a river, flows into the ocean, and then gets heated up and evaporates into the air, where it may become a cloud and start the process all over again. What was, for a time, a cloud is transformed into something new. We don't say the cloud dies when it changes form into raindrops. Are we really any different from the cloud? When we die, our bodies change form as they decompose and become part of nature, but they never cease to exist. Buddhists believe that humans, like everything else in nature, are part of a continual cycle of change.

You may have heard that the ultimate goal of Buddhism is to transcend this cycle and enter nirvana. That's true, but different sects interpret that idea in many different ways. For our purposes, it's enough to say there's an ongoing cycle of death and rebirth that we must understand before we even start to think about transcending it.

You're Dying, Too

A few years ago, my good friend and business partner taught me a wonderful lesson about life. He was diagnosed with stage 4 melanoma and was told he had only a few months to live. As his condition deteriorated, I asked him, "What does it feel like to know you're dying?" He just grinned at me and said, "You tell me! You're dying, too." He was right. We were both dying; we all are.

Buddhism teaches that thinking about death is a wise way to live. We don't need to spend our lives meditating in a cave to prepare for death, and we don't have to wait for the painful experience of losing someone we love (or even getting a terminal diagnosis ourselves) to shock us into living. We can begin here and now to make life meaningful by understanding that meaning isn't out there waiting to be found—it's in you, waiting to be created.

I like to use the following technique to keep death as an ever-present topic in my mind: Ask yourself, "What if I knew today was going to be my last day to live? How would that change my interactions with everyone I talk to today?" Then flip the question: "What if I knew that the person I'm talking to had only one more day to live? Would that change how I'm interacting with that person?"

Ardently do today
what must be done.
Who knows?
Tomorrow,
death comes.

THE BUDDHA,
THE BHADDEKARATTA SUTTA

Where does karma fit into all this? Doesn't Buddhism teach that what goes around comes around? Is karma a cosmic justice system?

Karma is one of the most well-known concepts from the Buddhist tradition, but it's also the most misunderstood. *Karma* (in Sanskrit) or *kamma* (in Pali) simply means "action." Most Westerners think of karma as some form of fate or cosmic justice—if you do something bad, the universe will eventually make something bad happen to you in response. The Buddhist understanding of karma is actually quite different. Karma is simply the law of cause and effect. There is no justice, intelligence, or moral system behind it, no punishment or reward. It's less "If I do something good, I will get something good" and more "If I do something, something will happen." Karma is not mysterious or hidden. It's the action that's taken, not the result.

When you begin to understand the nature of reality, that all things are interdependent and connected, you can start to see karma working all around you. For example, let's say someone gets into an argument with her coworker. Later, she drives home and, still upset, aggressively tailgates another car. The person being tailgated is now also upset, and when he arrives home to find his kids have spilled something on the floor, he yells at them. You can see how one act affects another act; this is karma in action. At any given moment, we're all acting upon the karma that has been set in motion by others. The central teaching of karma is that we can pause and break the cycle of reactivity. In that mindful pause, we have the freedom to choose a more skillful action to contribute to the never-ending web of causes and effects going on all around us.

Can you be agnostic or atheistic and still be Buddhist?

Buddhism is a nontheistic tradition, meaning there's no need to believe in a deity in order to follow or benefit from these teachings. There are some Buddhist cultural traditions that speak of gods, demons, and nonhuman beings with godlike characteristics, but there is no supreme creator God in any Buddhist teachings. The question of theism—whether a god or gods exist—is, quite frankly, irrelevant in Buddhism.

Perhaps a better approach to this question is to ask yourself, "Are my beliefs (or nonbeliefs) preventing me from seeing and experiencing reality properly?" Our minds are already full of beliefs, conclusions, judgments, and our own understanding of the "facts" of reality. We're usually far more interested in what we already think we know than in learning something new. If I believe there is a God, and in reality there isn't, no matter how obvious that is, I'll never see it, because I'm blinded by my belief that there is. Likewise, if I believe that God doesn't exist, God could be right in front of me and I wouldn't be able to see that because of my belief that there isn't a God.

Agnosticism, the stance that whether or not there's a God is ultimately unknowable, can play an important role on the path of awakening. In Buddhism, *not knowing* is an ideal mental state, because that's when we're open to learning and experiencing. Many Buddhists are agnostic not only about God but also about many of life's existential questions. This is what the Zen tradition calls a beginner's, or open, mind.

There's a story about a student who went to visit a famous Zen master, who quietly served tea as the student talked on and on about everything he knew about Zen. The master poured the student's cup to the brim, and then kept pouring. As the student watched the cup overflow, he blurted out, "It's full! No more will go in!"

"This is you," the master replied. "How can I show you Zen unless you first empty your cup?"

In a similar way, our beliefs—whether they're theist or atheistic—can blind us from seeing reality as it really is. But when we have a genuinely open mind, we have a sense of wonder and inquiry that allows us to learn something new, something we didn't even know that we didn't know.

What sets Buddhism apart from other major world religions? Can one be Buddhist and at the same time Christian, Jewish, or something else?

One of the key differences between Buddhism and other major religions is that while most other major religions focus on the answers to big existential questions (Who am I? Why am I here? What happens to me when I die? Is there a God or creative force behind everything?), Buddhism focuses on the questions themselves. It approaches the existential dilemmas of life by turning the question around and asking, "Why do I want to know the answer to these questions?" or "Who is the 'I' who wants to know who I am?" In that sense, Buddhism is not really at odds with other religions, because it doesn't present a set of answers that conflict with the answers other religions give. Additionally, while some religions focus on external sources of goodness and evil, like God and the devil, Buddhism holds that good and evil are found within and that the mind is the source of it all.

In the book *Buddhist Wisdom: The Path to Enlightenment*, the Dalai Lama is quoted as saying, "Do not try to use what you learn from Buddhism to be a Buddhist; use it to be a better whatever-you-already-are." I personally know Buddhists who are atheists, Buddhists who are Christians, and Buddhists who don't identify with any other ideological or religious label. Buddhism can be practiced somewhat like yoga: as something you do, not something you *are*.

*Both formerly and now,
it is only suffering
that I describe,
and the cessation
of suffering.*

**THE BUDDHA,
THE SUTTA NIPATA**

This is all really interesting, but it gets a little abstract. How can these Buddhist concepts make a difference in my day-to-day life?

A couple of years ago, my wife gave birth to our third child, a baby girl. When I finally got to hold her, I was instantly flooded with emotions, and suddenly I found myself thinking about all my hopes and dreams for her. I was looking into her eyes, imagining what she'd look like, what her sense of humor would be like, and what she would be when she grew up. Then, in the next moment, I had another thought: What if she gets sick? My thoughts started to race as I pictured her with tubes in her nose and needles in her arms.

But then I thought about the impermanent nature of each moment and of life itself. I was able to pause the reactive thinking and just be present with her. I stared into her little eyes and enjoyed the moment. I knew there was no certainty about what tomorrow would bring, but I was certain that in that moment, I was experiencing something indescribable. I was experiencing the present, a moment that has never been and will never be again. It felt like pure magic!

We live life moment by moment, with uncertainty our only certainty because the present moment is all we'll ever have. This includes happy moments, sad moments, moments when we feel anger or compassion. They're all just moments, completely unique and precious. Buddhist concepts and teachings can help us stay anchored in the present, whether it's a magical moment like the one I had with my daughter or an ordinary moment just sitting at a red light. They all can be moments of profound awareness when we see them the right way. Buddhist concepts and teachings offer the tools to find greater freedom, meaning, and peace in your day-to-day experience of being alive.

PART 3

CORE TEACHINGS

What You'll Learn: In this section, you'll learn about key Buddhist teachings, such as the Four Noble Truths and the Eightfold Path. They may sound intimidating, but we'll discuss how and why anyone can benefit from putting these teachings into action in their everyday lives.

If Buddhism were to be summarized in one key teaching, what would it be?

The essence of the Buddha's teaching is the nature of suffering and the cessation of suffering. In an early Buddhist text, the Buddha is reported to have said, "Both formerly and now, it is only suffering that I describe, and the cessation of suffering" (Saṃyutta Nikāya 22.86). One of the first teachings that the Buddha gave after realizing enlightenment was that of the Four Noble Truths. Each of the truths relates in some way to suffering, which is an inescapable part of life. The Four Noble Truths are: the truth of suffering (*dukkha*), the truth of the cause of suffering (*samudaya*), the truth of the end of suffering (*nirodha*), and the truth of the path that leads to the end of suffering (*magga*).

You can think of the Four Noble Truths in terms of a medical practice, wherein a doctor (the Buddha) diagnoses the problem (suffering), identifies the underlying causes, determines the prognosis, and finally prescribes a course of treatment. The Four Noble Truths are meant to be an action plan for dealing with the inevitable suffering that humanity experiences. In this sense, they can be viewed as tasks rather than truths. They're meant to be four tasks we *do* rather than four truths we *believe*. When I interviewed him on my podcast, Buddhist scholar and author Stephen Batchelor discussed the Four Noble Truths as tasks with an easy-to-remember acronym: ELSA.

E - Embrace the instance of suffering.

L - Let go of the reactive pattern.

S - See the stopping of the reactivity.

A - Act skillfully.

The teaching of the Four Noble Truths forms the core of all Buddhist paths, schools, and traditions. The essence of the Four Noble Truths is to address and embrace the truth of human suffering.

What does it mean to embrace suffering? Suffering sucks, so how are we supposed to do that? In other words, what's the deal with the first noble truth?

The first of the Four Noble Truths, known in Pali as *dukkha*, recognizes the presence of suffering in life. This first noble truth diagnoses the problem": In life, difficulties arise, and we suffer. It's not a matter of if, but when. Sickness, old age, and death are some of the most obvious examples, but there are countless difficulties in life, from losing your job to dropping your phone and cracking the screen.

The nature of reality is that difficulties will arise, and we'll experience suffering. We can begin to embrace that fact by recognizing that suffering in general is not personal. It's simply part of the experience of existence. And we *will* experience suffering, no matter how hard we try to avoid it. Whether we search for a magic formula to remove it, chase after money to buy it off, or seek fame to drown it out; no matter if we pray, meditate, or perform rituals to shield ourselves from it; suffering, in some form, will find us. It is the central problem of human existence.

This diagnosis is universal. It's not just you; it's all of us. The rich, the famous, the powerful, the pious—everyone! If you think you're alone with your difficulties, spend some time talking to others and ask them about their problems. You'll soon discover that everyone has struggles and pain to contend with.

What we learn from the Buddha about embracing suffering is that life is going to be easier for us when we truly accept that suffering is a part of life for *everyone*; there's no way around it.

Through the Woods

Imagine you're going on a hike through the woods. You're enjoying the sights and sounds, maybe stopping occasionally to admire a bit of birdsong or take a picture of a particularly lovely flower. Then, suddenly, as you're strolling serenely along, a bear jumps out of the bushes directly at you, roaring loudly. You're probably screaming in fear for your very life, trying desperately to think of a way to save yourself, bitterly regretting the decision to go on this hike, wondering what will happen to your children. "Why me?" you may think. "Why this?" But then, let's say the bear stands up and takes off its head. It isn't really a bear; it's just a guy in a bear costume trying to scare hikers.

Now imagine taking that hike again, but this time, before you go, I warn you that someone is hiding along the path, dressed in a bear costume and jumping out to scare people. Now that you know, you'll be on the look-out. Of course, the hike is long, and at times you forget. The moment the guy in the bear costume jumps out to scare you, you'll still be startled. You might even jump or scream. But you won't be completely terrorized, and you'll recover from the shock more quickly, because you were forewarned and had some time to accept the idea that someone was going to jump out at you. You'll say to yourself, "I knew this was going to happen at some point. It's happened to lots of other hikers."

This is essentially what Buddhism teaches us about suffering. It's there, and it's scary, and at some point it's going to jump out and startle you, but it doesn't have to utterly terrify you. Try this: The next time you experience suffering or distress, instead of saying, "Life's not fair" or, "Why is this happening to me?" tell yourself, "I was aware that this could happen. I'm not alone. Others are also experiencing this same thing." Once you know that suffering is an unavoidable part of the experience, you can embrace the fact that it will happen at some point, worry less about it, and be prepared to recover more quickly when it comes.

Even "acceptance" seems like a lot to ask. Are we also supposed to just accept all the bad things happening in the world?

The purpose of Buddhist teachings is to try to help us better understand the nature of reality and gain a clearer understanding of how things really are. Acceptance, from the Buddhist perspective, is not about giving up or ignoring bad things, like injustice or suffering. Acceptance in the Buddhist sense is about not resisting or fighting against reality. For example, if you're feeling a certain emotion—let's say, loneliness—you have to accept what it is you're feeling before you can do something about it. If you shy away from acknowledging that you're lonely and instead ignore the uncomfortable feeling, anything you do to alleviate that discomfort will be unsuccessful, because you're aiming at the wrong target.

I think we sometimes equate acceptance with resignation or giving up, but acceptance is not the same as resignation. Several years ago, I was dealing with a difficult situation in my life. I experienced a breach of trust from someone very close to me, and I was upset and hurt. But at the time, I felt that I shouldn't be angry. I felt like it was my responsibility to "accept" what happened and get over it. This attitude only aggravated the situation, and I probably remained angry about what had happened longer than I otherwise would have. It wasn't until several years later that I learned what acceptance really was. I had never fully accepted how I felt—I had just pretended to. In reality I was angry about the situation, and I was angry that I felt angry. I didn't accept how I was feeling, thus prolonging my own pain.

Upon discovering this, I decided that I was finally ready to accept not the breach of trust but the fact of my own anger. I was angry, and that was perfectly okay. It felt so liberating to accept my emotions and stop resisting what I was feeling. This marked the beginning of my healing journey, and it all started with accepting my reality and giving up the fight against it. From the Buddhist perspective, it's not that we're accepting the bad things that happen; we're just accepting *that* bad things happen. Once I accept the reality of a situation, I can ask, "Now what am I going to do about it?" Acceptance is about working with reality, not against it.

Tell me about the second noble truth. You're saying the way to reduce suffering is to become less reactive to difficult things that happen to us, but that's really hard! How do we let go of that reactivity?

The second truth, *samudaya*, addresses the cause of suffering. The main cause of our suffering is the way we habitually react to life as it unfolds: telling ourselves stories that ascribe meaning to events, wondering why painful things happen to us, wishing things were different, and so on. Suffering emerges when we want life to be different—when we struggle against what is. We get frustrated when the world doesn't behave the way we think it should, and this causes us to suffer and then react.

Experiencing suffering isn't the real problem, however. The problem arises in how we react to that suffering. The Buddha taught that "when touched with a feeling of pain, the ordinary uninstructed person sorrows, grieves, and laments, beats his breast, becomes distraught. So he feels two pains, physical and mental. Just as if they were to shoot a man with an arrow and, right afterward, were to shoot him with another one, so that he would feel the pains of two arrows" (Saṃyutta Nikāya 36.6). Reactivity becomes a vicious cycle. The more we dwell on our sense of suffering, the more we reinforce the very cause of it: wanting life to be other than it is. The more intense the suffering, the more we want to be rid of it. But the more we want to be rid of it, the more intense the suffering will be.

Anyone who's ever punched a hole in the wall or said something in anger and later regretted it has experienced reactivity. The emotional discomfort of suffering can be so great that it seems the only logical next step is to react to the discomfort of it—by, for example, punching the wall. Letting go of reactivity is letting go of the need to punch the wall, the need to react to our suffering in rage or despair that only creates more suffering when we have to, say, get stitches or repair a hole in the wall.

Ceasing reactivity doesn't mean we need to let go of the discomfort that makes us feel like punching the wall. (That's not really possible, in any case.) Letting go of reactivity is about avoiding the second arrow. It's more an act of liberation than a sacrifice we have to make. Eventually we come to understand that letting go of pain is no sacrifice at all.

That does sound like a better way to deal with life, but is it realistic? Is it really possible to end suffering? What does the third noble truth say?

As mentioned before, we suffer when we crave for life to be other than it is. The third noble truth, *nirodha*, helps us understand that in the cessation of suffering, it's not suffering that ceases, but rather our craving *not to suffer*.

Buddhist practice doesn't end suffering; suffering is a lifelong reality. But we can let go of our attachment to avoiding suffering, which paradoxically causes us so much avoidable suffering. This is a tricky concept to grasp, because we can't do away with our craving to not suffer by simple force of will. In fact, when we try to no longer cling to it, we're clinging to the idea of not clinging. If we desire to not desire, we're still caught by desire. We can't just say, "Okay, from now on, I won't cling to anything," because the causes and conditions that give rise to clinging will still be present.

My twin brother once called to tell me of an experience he had. He was driving on the highway when suddenly, like in the example on page 6, someone cut him off. He was instantly aware of his emotional reaction and the anger he was feeling inside, and as he observed the emotion he was experiencing, he asked himself, "Is the observer of the emotion also angry?" In that moment, he was able to distinguish between the emotion he was experiencing and the observation of the emotion.

That pause allowed him to stop and see the reactivity that was unfolding. In that moment, the emotion of anger no longer had a grip on him. He was able to see the emotion and to allow it just to *be*. He was experiencing the emotion of anger, yes, but he was not reacting to it; he was never shot by the "second arrow" of suffering.

Since the fourth noble truth is the path that leads to the end of suffering, how do we start down that path?

The last of the Four Noble Truths is *magga*, Pali for "path." From the moment the Buddha realized his enlightenment, all his teachings dealt with this path in one way or another. It may have been explained differently to different people according to where they were on their own individual paths of awakening, but the essence of the Buddha's many discourses and teachings can be found in the Eightfold Path, often referred to as the Path of Liberation or the path to the cessation of suffering. The eight parts of the path can be grouped into three essential categories of Buddhist practice: wisdom (*paññā*), ethical conduct (*sīla*), and mental discipline (*samādhi*). The Eightfold Path isn't meant to be followed in sequential order; all eight areas are developed simultaneously in an ongoing way. They're all linked in the sense that each one helps with the cultivation of others. The eight parts of the path, grouped by their three categories, are:

WISDOM

1. Right understanding (*sammā diṭṭhi*)
2. Right intent (*sammā saṅkappa*)

ETHICAL CONDUCT

3. Right speech (*sammā vācā*)
4. Right action (*sammā kammanta*)
5. Right livelihood (*sammā ājīva*)

6. Right effort (*sammā vāyāma*)
7. Right mindfulness (*sammā sati*)
8. Right concentration (*sammā samādhi*)

The Eightfold Path is not a path we walk only once or in a particular order. You'll notice how various segments of the path overlap and rely on each other and how some of them flow into or relate back to each other, as well. It's also not a moral code to be followed. The components have the word *right* in them, but don't think of these in terms of right versus wrong. Instead, think of them as wise or skillful ways of living. The Eightfold Path is meant to be a guide for specific areas of life in which we can experience and discover the true nature of reality. "Walking the path" is an ongoing practice that can bring about a new sense of awareness and perspective in our lives.

Every Day Is a Good Day

I have a scroll hanging in my office with five Chinese characters written in calligraphy, *Nichi nichi kore kō jitsu*, which means "Every day is a good day." It can be a powerful reminder of life's interdependent nature when I realize I'm focusing too much on myself and my own suffering.

My brother and I both enjoy paragliding as a hobby, and though we live far away from each other, we like to meet up and fly from time to time. Once, we planned a trip to a favorite flying site of mine near Sand City, California, where, when the winds are right, you can soar along the coast above the sand dunes for miles at a time. This was going to be his first time flying at this location, so I was eager for him to share this incredible experience of soaring over the sand dunes. I arrived a day early, and the winds were great. The next morning, I picked him up at the airport, and we drove out to the launch site . . . and ended up sitting there for four hours waiting for the wind to pick up. It never did, and it remained calm for the next several days. We never got to fly.

I was disappointed and frustrated that my brother didn't get the chance to fly (and that he had used up his frequent-flier miles to get there). It seemed like an unfortunate series of days for us. But later that week, we saw on the news that the calm winds had allowed firefighters to contain one of the huge wildfires raging through California at the time. I thought to myself, "Every day is a good day."

Let's start with the section related to wisdom. What does it mean to have right understanding?

Right, or wise, understanding starts by simply recognizing that what we're seeing might not actually be what it appears to be. Imagine walking into a barn, seeing a coiled hose, and mistaking it for a snake. You wouldn't be experiencing reality but rather the picture of reality in your head. You might immediately react as though there really were a snake, giving a startled gasp or turning and running away, yet the reality is that there is no snake. Wisdom is like turning on the light in the barn and revealing that the snake is actually a hose. We must continually seek wisdom to help us learn to see the world as it really is. The Four Noble Truths and the three marks of existence (suffering, impermanence, and nonself) help us have a wise understanding of the nature of reality. The wisdom of understanding is not about acquiring more knowledge. In fact, it's the opposite: It's about trying to unlearn the concepts and ideas that prevent us from seeing reality as it is.

What does it mean to have right intent?

If we want to reduce suffering, we need to be aware of the intentions we have regarding the things we say and do. When our intentions stem from anger or hatred, they're more likely to cause harm than if they stem from happiness or gratitude. When we behave reactively, it is very difficult to be mindful of the intent behind our words and actions. It takes practice to become aware of our intentions. You can start this practice by asking yourself, "Why?" as you react to things in life. When I'm feeling anger, for example, I like to ask myself, "Why am I experiencing this emotion?" If I'm being kind to someone, I ask myself, "Why? Is it because I genuinely care about this person, or am I trying to gain something out of this interaction?" When you become aware of your intentions, you can decide if you need to create new intentions and perhaps let go of the old ones. This will cause you to speak and act more skillfully.

Moving on to the ethical conduct section of the Eightfold Path, what does it mean to have right speech?

The way we communicate with ourselves and others is an essential part of creating a peaceful and harmonious life. We are social creatures, and communication is the most important part of human relations. Right speech means communicating with others in a way that doesn't cause harm. (And, yes, this includes all forms of communication—writing, texting, e-mailing, even Facebook.) Lying, gossiping, or insulting others is not right speech, but neither are compliments you don't mean, promises you don't intend to keep, or sucking up to someone you want to impress. With right speech, you consider why you say something as much as what you say.

Consider the difference between constructive criticism and destructive criticism. The former may be hard to hear, but its goal is to help you become better at what you're doing. The latter is intended only to cause pain. Right speech doesn't always have to be pleasant, nor does it need to withhold ideas out of fear that someone might disagree, but it should be sincere and genuine.

What does right action mean? Is it a set of rules to follow?

Right action or conduct means doing what is proper and necessary for your situation. While this sometimes includes (and certainly doesn't discourage) a sense of "doing the right thing" morally, it more closely resembles a guideline for behaving appropriately in any situation. The problem with a set moral code is that morals change and evolve over time and are different in different cultures. Adhering to the moral code of another place and time may not be the wisest form of action for our place and time.

There's a quote popularly attributed to H. L. Mencken: "Morality is doing what's right regardless of what you're told. Obedience is doing what you're told regardless of what's right." Right action is not, in other words, a set of rules to be followed to the letter in every situation. How could it be, when life is continually changing and evolving? Ideally, right understanding, right thinking, and right speech give rise to right action, your wisdom leading you to behave fittingly in any scenario.

Should a person do good,
let him do it
again and again.
Let him find pleasure
therein,
for blissful is
the accumulation
of good.

THE BUDDHA,
THE DHAMMAPADA

What does right livelihood mean? Does Buddhism consider certain jobs better than others?

Livelihood is how we make a living and how we interact with others while on the job. We each need to determine for ourselves if what we do for a living is doing more harm or good for ourselves and others. You may be thinking, "Okay, drug dealers do harm and doctors do good," but this Buddhist teaching goes beyond just the type of job or career we have. It also includes how we interact with our coworkers or customers. It would not be right livelihood if a doctor were causing harm by taking bribes from a pharmaceutical company to prescribe a certain medicine over another. Ultimately, it's up to us to make the judgment call regarding the way we make a living. It's a good idea to incorporate right intent in this determination process. Try asking yourself, "Why am I doing what I'm doing?" Remember, right livelihood is not necessarily about picking a job with the Red Cross or some other humanitarian cause. It's about doing what you do with the best intent not to cause harm, regardless of what your job is.

I used to work for a company that sold health supplements, but after a while, I became really uncomfortable with one of the sales methods we used with our customers. We would entice them to try the supplement by signing them up for a free trial, and then they would be automatically enrolled in a monthly subscription for the supplement that they were often unaware of. While I believed in the product itself, I was very uncomfortable with the harm and frustration we were causing to so many people who weren't reading the fine print when signing up for their free trial. For me, this job was not a form of right livelihood. I ended up leaving that job and finding another, where I no longer had conflicting feelings about my livelihood.

Tell me about the Eightfold Path's view of mental discipline. What does it mean to have right effort? Does it mean trying harder to be better?

Right effort is what it takes to put into practice all the other parts of the path. It takes effort on our part if we want to experience any kind of positive change in our lives. In order to learn a new skill—in music, sports, business, or anything else—we must apply effort. Without it, we usually make little to no progress. In the same way, right effort affects everything we do in the world.

I've been trying to learn to play guitar for over 10 years, but I've never actually mastered it, because I've had a hard time putting in the effort required to practice. I've put time and effort into other things that I've wanted to accomplish (like writing this book!), but the guitar remains difficult for me. Luckily, not being able to play guitar well hasn't had a huge impact on my life. But sometimes we feel this way about more important things—like jobs, relationships, or the way we live in the world—and don't put enough effort in. Right effort is about dedicating the time and work required to become more mindful and aware of the nature of reality. Without that effort, there can be no awakening or enlightenment.

What does it mean to have right mindfulness? Is this about meditating?

Right mindfulness is about paying attention, whether we're meditating or just going about our daily tasks. Being mindful helps us stay anchored in the present moment, which keeps us in touch with reality as it is. Zen master Thich Nhat Hanh describes mindfulness like this: "When you have a toothache, the feeling is very unpleasant, and when you do not have a toothache, you usually have a neutral feeling. However, if you can be mindful of the non-toothache, the non-toothache will become a feeling of peace and joy. Mindfulness gives rise to and nourishes happiness." In this sense, mindfulness helps us become aware that at any given moment, we are capable of experiencing contentment. It's just a matter of increasing our sphere of awareness to notice all the "non-toothaches" we're currently experiencing.

What is right concentration? Is it about sitting and focusing on something? Is this the goal of meditation?

Right, or wise, concentration is the practice of focusing the mind solely on one thing: whatever it is we're doing at that moment. Meditation is a great tool to practice concentration. When we think of meditation, we typically think of sitting cross-legged on the floor with our eyes closed, and that's definitely one way to practice, but meditation can be much more than just sitting. We can practice meditation while washing the dishes, walking, or doing virtually any other activity.

The opposite of right concentration is distraction. Whether it's the chime on our smartphones indicating that a new text has arrived or one of thousands of advertisements competing for our attention, distraction is everywhere. Distraction prevents us from seeing life as it really is, from seeing the truth about ourselves and others. One day, I decided to ride my bike to work instead of driving, and while rounding a bend in the road, I noticed a red barn behind a cluster of trees out in a field. I had driven past this exact spot almost daily for years, focusing on driving, distracted by the radio or thoughts about work, and I'd never noticed that red barn. But on this day, going slowly and paying attention, I discovered something new that had been there all along. How many things are waiting to be discovered or seen when we simply pay attention and stay aware?

Mushrooms

When I was growing up, I remember having to sit at the dinner table until all the food on my plate was gone. Because I was a picky eater, this was a difficult task, and when mushrooms were on the table, I knew I'd be sitting there for a very long time. I thought to myself at those times, "I hate mushrooms." I didn't like the flavor, texture, color, or anything else about them. But as I got older, I developed a taste for mushrooms. Now they're one of my favorite things to eat. I now recognize that it was never "I" who loved or hated mushrooms; it was my taste buds and my nose conspiring to give me the experience that "I" hated mushrooms. The average person has about 10,000 taste buds, and they're continually being replaced by new ones. As we get older, things begin to taste different to us. Because of the impermanent, constantly changing nature of the body, I don't even know what foods I will or won't enjoy in the next 5, 10, or 20 years. Being aware of this allows me to try foods that I previously thought "I" disliked.

Next time you eat a meal, whether it's one of your favorite foods or something you think you hate, remind yourself that it's not "you" who likes or dislikes certain things. It's your sense organs, along with mental formations and everything else happening in your mind, that leave you with that perception. And perceptions, like a taste for mushrooms, can change.

It seems like "I" am the source of a lot of important things—awareness, suffering, "good," and "evil." What else can Buddhism teach me about the nature of myself? What makes me *me*?

According to Buddhist teachings, our "self" is a perspective—it is a product of our perception. Our sense of self is an event that occurs rather than a thing that exists. Imagine pausing a movie to see a single still image. Every film is made up of those individual frames, but when we watch movies, we perceive them as one continuous moving image telling a connected story. Our selves are like the filmstrip: a collection of unique still frames that are generated in each moment-to-moment experience of being alive. If you could pause time and see the individual frame in this specific moment, you would see that it's slightly different from the ones just before and after it. In other words, the you of right now is not the same you of the previous moment.

The Buddha taught that we are made up of five components that come together to create the perception of a distinct, individual "I" or "me." These five components are called the five *skandhas*, a Sanskrit word meaning "aggregates" or "heaps." The five aggregates (and their original Pali titles) are form (*rūpa*), sensation (*vedanā*), perception (*saññā*), mental formations or thoughts (*saṅkhāra*), and consciousness (*viññāṇa*).

On this subject, the Buddha furthermore taught that we sense reality and our world through six sense organs. The eyes sense visible form, the ears sense sound, the nose senses odor, the tongue senses taste, the body senses tangible things, and the mind senses thoughts or ideas. (You'll notice that the first five senses are the ones we're all taught in school, but Buddhism also considers the mind to be a sense organ, since our minds sense thoughts and ideas.)

Tell me more about these five aggregates. How do they work?

The five aggregates that give rise to the sense of self are:

FORM OR MATERIALITY (RŪPA)

Form or matter is simply something material that can be sensed with one of the five conventional senses, like sight, sound, or taste.

SENSATION OR FEELING TONE (VEDANĀ)

This is the feeling state that arises when we sense something. When we smell something, we immediately develop a "feeling tone" around what was sensed—pleasant or unpleasant, desirable or undesirable. The feeling tones associated with the senses can be understood as sensations of pleasure, pain, or neutrality.

PERCEPTION (SAÑÑĀ)

This is the recognition or identification of a sensation we've experienced. When we see something, we start scanning our memories to try to find anything that might be associated with what we're perceiving. For example, a dark hallway will produce a sense of discomfort for many people based on context or past memories (even if only of a scary movie). Perception is the process of giving names, like "dark," "hallway," and "scary," to what we're sensing.

MENTAL FORMATION OR THOUGHT PROCESSES (SAŊKHĀRA)

This is where our likes, dislikes, biases, and prejudices come in. If I smell a block of pungent cheese, my mental formations affect the perception I have of it in that moment. The smell of the cheese may remind me of a trip to France, or it may remind me of my old roommate's stinky feet. Either way, my mental formations will alter my perception of smelling the cheese. Mental formations always precede the mental states we experience.

CONSCIOUSNESS OR AWARENESS (VIÑÑĀŅA)

Consciousness is the general awareness of each of the other aggregates that makes the entire process of experience possible. For example, when we see a book sitting on a table, our eyes and the book don't produce an experience by themselves. Only the co-arising of consciousness, the eyes, the book, and the rest of the aggregates produces the experience of seeing. This is why, in Buddhism, we often refer to consciousness based on a specific sense organ. So when you see a sight, eye-consciousness arises; when you hear a sound, ear-consciousness arises. Once we're aware of this relationship between the sense organ and what is being sensed through awareness, we notice that there's an emotional response taking place. When we're sensing, we're actually engaging with the object being sensed on an emotional level.

So how do these senses and perceptions make me *me*?

Our sense of self is created by our emotional responses to what we're perceiving in each moment. The moment we see, hear, smell, taste, feel, or think something, the sensation of a "self" that senses emerges. In other words, perception happens and immediately gives rise to the awareness of the perception. The "I" that is aware of the perception taking place gives rise to the sense of self.

The Buddha incorporated the five aggregates into many of his other teachings. The most important point he made about these teachings is that the aggregates that combine to make you experience "you" are not actually you. They are temporary, interdependent, conditional phenomena, and the idea of these perceived and experienced aggregates being you is an illusion.

When we realize that these aggregates are just temporary phenomena, conditional and created by other phenomena—that they're *not us*—then we're on the path to enlightenment.

Whatever is not yours, abandon it. What is it that is not yours? Material form, feeling, perception, formations, consciousness. These are not yours. When you have abandoned them, that will lead to your welfare and happiness for a long time.

THE BUDDHA, MAJJHIMA NIKĀYA

PART 4

CORE
PRACTICES

What You'll Learn: In this section, you'll learn about some of the common ways that Buddhist practitioners apply the teachings and concepts from the first three parts. You'll gain a better understanding about why and how these practices can benefit anyone who uses them, whether they're Buddhist or not. You don't have to become a Buddhist to recognize the wisdom and transformational power of these ways of experiencing and interacting with the world and people around you.

There seems to be a certain lifestyle that sometimes goes with Buddhism, like nonviolence and not being materialistic. Where does that come from?

Many religions have a formal set of moral or ethical rules, like the Ten Commandments, that are usually prescribed by an authorative figure, like the Judeo-Christian God. Buddhism doesn't have a god or a list of commandments that Buddhists are compelled to obey, but it does have a set of five basic precepts, or rules, that most practicing Buddhists strive to follow. The precepts are not command-ments; they're better understood as recommendations for a way of living a more harmonious life. The end goal of the precepts is to practice a lifestyle that harmonizes our actions with reality as it is.

What are these precepts? How do they instruct Buddhists to live?

The discipline of following the precepts in your life is part of the path to enlightenment, because it is believed that a person who is enlightened would naturally be living by the precepts. The five precepts are as follows:

1. ABSTAIN FROM TAKING LIFE.

There are no moral absolutes in Buddhism, so this precept, along with the others, may be interpreted differently from one person or tradition to another. For some people, this precept may inform a stance on abortion, capital punishment, or the killing of insects. In order to properly weigh the consequences of our actions, it's helpful to examine whether our actions are motivated by greed, hatred, and delusion or by kindness, wisdom, and compassion. Intent plays a key role here. If my family is being attacked by a bear, for example, I may have to take the life of the bear to save the lives of those being threatened. If the killing is done without hatred, it can be interpreted as being in accordance with this precept.

2. ABSTAIN FROM TAKING WHAT IS NOT GIVEN.

The precepts of Buddhism are closely associated with right action, part of the Eightfold Path discussed on page 84. Abstaining from taking what is not given seems natural enough, but this precept goes beyond just not stealing. It includes evaluating your own motivations and understanding how your actions will affect others. Abstaining from taking what is not given can also be a source of happiness or contentment. For example, we may feel a sense of joy in knowing that we have not harmed others by stealing from them. We can also feel a sense of joy in knowing that others trust us and our word. There is peace and joy in living a life of no remorse.

3. ABSTAIN FROM SEXUAL MISCONDUCT.

This precept is also understood differently across the various schools of Buddhism. In some schools of Buddhism, like Theravada, monks and nuns are celibate, while in other schools, like Japan's Jōdo Shinshū, marriage is common and acceptable for clergy members. What constitutes misconduct will be determined by the inherited culture and societal views of different Buddhist practitioners. It's safe to say that things like nonconsensual sex and sexual exploitation definitely fall under the label of misconduct, but the adherence of other actions to this precept may vary by school and cultural background. As with all the precepts, examining how an action will make you feel and how it will impact others is a good starting point for determining if an action is in alignment with this rule.

4. ABSTAIN FROM INCORRECT SPEECH.

This precept goes beyond not telling lies, although that's a part of it. It means speaking honestly and communicating in a way that is beneficial to others. Incorrect speech is speech that is rooted in the three poisons of greed, hatred, and ignorance. Misleading others in your communication just to get what you want, speaking in a way that is intentionally hurtful to others, and gossiping are all forms of incorrect speech. Correct speech arises naturally when we're speaking without greed, hatred, or delusion.

5. ABSTAIN FROM INTOXICANTS THAT CLOUD THE MIND.

This precept is interpreted and practiced differently in the various schools of Buddhism. For some Buddhists, this precept is understood to be a strict prohibition of intoxicating substances, like drugs and alcohol; for others, "intoxicants" can be anything that clouds the mind or alters perception. This may include the media we consume or even "intoxicating" addictive habits, like gambling. This precept is meant to encourage practitioners to be cautious about the things that distract us from having a direct experience of life.

One is not called noble
who harms living beings.
By not harming living beings
one is called noble.

THE BUDDHA,
THE DHAMMAPADA

Are Buddhists vegetarians? Is it possible to be Buddhist and also eat meat?

Some Buddhists are vegetarians, and some are not. Again, there's nothing mandatory to do or refrain from doing in order to be a Buddhist. The Buddha did not require his followers to be vegetarians; while he taught that killing was an unskillful practice, he also encouraged monks to graciously accept whatever food was offered to them, including meat.

Some schools of Buddhism encourage and practice a vegetarian diet as a way to follow the first precept, but others don't. Some will argue that in order to abstain from killing, one must be a vegetarian, while others point out that many animals, like worms and insects, die in the process of plowing fields and spraying crops to produce vegetarian food. In the end, it's a personal choice, and each person must decide if vegetarianism is suitable for his or her particular circumstances in life.

Is there similar room for interpretation of the fifth precept about intoxicants? Do many Buddhists drink alcohol anyway?

Once again, some do and some don't—that's what happens when there are no absolute mandates! While the fifth precept is about avoiding intoxicants that cloud the mind, it doesn't necessarily mean that alcohol is prohibited. Some schools of Buddhism will suggest avoiding alcohol completely, while others will suggest not drinking past the point of being mindful.

As with any action, it's important to understand the intent behind one's drinking. Some people drink as a form of escaping their reality rather than confronting it, understanding it, and accepting it. From the Buddhist perspective, that's an unskillful approach to life that can cause unnecessary suffering to oneself and others. One of the main objectives of Buddhist practice is to gain greater insight into the nature of one's own mind, and this task is nearly impossible when the mind is clouded. (It's hard to do even when you're totally sober!)

So Buddhism doesn't necessarily consider drinking a moral issue per se, but clouding our minds or judgment with alcohol or drugs isn't generally seen as moving closer to enlightenment. The question of whether to abstain entirely from alcohol or just drink in moderation is a personal decision that requires self-reflection, honesty, and maturity to answer.

Do you have to become a Buddhist to practice Buddhism? How do you become a Buddhist?

Buddhism is not a proselytizing religion, which means it's not really focused on or interested in converting anyone to anything. If Buddhist concepts and teachings make sense to you, you can begin to put them into practice in your own life. Anyone can benefit from them—you don't have to formally "become a Buddhist."

However, if you do decide that Buddhism is the right path for you, you can do what is called taking refuge in the *tisarana* (the "three refuges," also known as the "three jewels"): the Buddha, the dharma ("teachings"), and the *sangha* ("community"). Most forms of Buddhism do this with a formal ceremony at a Buddhist temple, but it can also be done on a personal level by simply reciting, "I take refuge in the Buddha. I take refuge in the dharma. I take refuge in the *sangha*."

Tell me more about the three refuges. What does it really mean to "take refuge" in these things?

In a literal sense, *taking refuge* means finding shelter or protection from danger. The danger we face is that of being controlled by our own habitual reactivity and unskillful thoughts. The idea is that, by seeking a safe place in these resources, we will minimize or even eliminate the suffering we cause to ourselves and others by being habitually reactive. I like to think of the process of taking refuge as similar to making a New Year's resolution, where we set an intention to be better than we've been in the past. Let's take a closer look at what each of these refuges mean.

"I take refuge in the Buddha." To seek shelter in the Buddha means to recognize that the Buddha was capable of attaining enlightenment, and, therefore, so are we. Taking refuge in the Buddha is an invitation to see ourselves in him and to strive to attain liberation from our own habitual reactivity and the poisons of greed, hatred, and ignorance in our own minds.

"I take refuge in the dharma." To seek safety in Buddhist teachings is to recognize that they can give us a new perspective and a profound understanding of ourselves and the nature of reality. It goes beyond just trusting or accepting the teachings. It's about trusting that our practice of the teachings will indeed create a more peaceful and harmonious way of living.

"I take refuge in the sangha." To seek refuge in the Buddhist community is to recognize that, by practicing with others, we can find and offer support. The importance of practicing with others cannot be overestimated. A good friend helps us see the unskillful actions that we may not see in ourselves. Opening ourselves up to others and allowing them to support us while we simultaneously support them is a critical step to overcoming an ego-centered life.

Everybody talks about meditating, and the Buddha found enlightenment through meditation, so it seems like an important practice. But how do you do it? Is there a correct Buddhist way?

There are countless meditation techniques and methods taught among the various schools of Buddhism. (And some schools of Buddhism don't practice meditation at all.) One of the most common techniques is mindfulness meditation. The goal of this technique is to learn to become an observer of the world and our own experiences. We spend so much of our time in thinking mode, ascribing meaning to our thoughts and emotions. We chase after thoughts with other thoughts or try to control our thoughts, which only aggravates the overall problem of being habitually reactive. Mindfulness meditation helps us break out of this cycle of reactivity.

The technique can be as simple as observing your breath. Notice what it feels like to breathe. Can you feel the slight temperature fluctuations at the tip of your nose between the in-breath and the out-breath? Do you notice the subtle rise and fall in your chest, shoulders, or abdomen with each breath? When we observe, we pause our reactive thinking and stop making up meaning. For example, when we're sitting outside watching the clouds float by, we don't have the tendency to ascribe value to the shapes we see. We don't think, "This is a good cloud" or "That's a bad cloud," "That cloud isn't puffy enough," or

"That cloud is too tall." In these moments of observation, we just see the cloud for what it is. When we turn this process inward, we can start to experience the same unbiased, nonjudgmental attitude toward our own thoughts and feelings. Suddenly we're not judging our anger as good or bad. We just notice that we're experiencing an emotion and allow it to remain without resisting it or trying to fight it off. Before we know it, the emotion will dissipate or be replaced by another, just like the clouds in the sky.

Looking at a River

I live in a mountainous region, and I enjoy spending time hiking various mountain trails in the summer. A few summers back, I was hiking up a trail that overlooks a river, and I paused there to relax and meditate. After my meditation, I looked at the river and watched the water continually flowing downstream. I thought about how there is really no permanent aspect of that river. The water is always new; the banks are continually changing and evolving as the sediment and rocks wash away and erode; the path of the river changes at different times of the year depending on how much water is flowing down. The river itself is always new, always changing.

I then connected this observation with what I had just been observing as I looked inward in meditation. What part of me is permanent? My cells are continually regenerating and splitting. My older memories are fading, while new memories are always being added. My thoughts, ideas, and opinions seem to be continually evolving over time. I realized that, like the river, I myself seem like a permanent thing, yet there is nothing permanent to be found when I look for it. Meditation can bring about a profound shift in perspective when we learn to look deeply at something. Something as simple as looking at a river can help us find the universal laws of interdependence and impermanence within and without us.

I once heard that the goal of meditation is to have a totally blank mind. Am I supposed to stop thinking when I meditate?

The idea that meditation requires a blank mind is a common misconception. When we meditate, we're simply trying to observe what's there—thoughts, emotions, everything. Trying to control our thoughts—or anything else—is actually one of the major contributors to suffering, because we experience suffering the moment we want things to be other than they are. We do this regularly with our own thoughts. I have a thought, I find it unpleasant, and I try to forcibly remove that thought from my mind. But the thought of removing the unpleasant thought only reinforces it.

So the goal of meditation isn't to control our thoughts; it's to observe them and become more familiar with the inner workings of our minds. Try it, and see what happens when you stop attempting to control your thoughts. Notice how thoughts, like all other things, are interdependent and impermanent. Thoughts arise, linger, and then dissipate or get replaced by other thoughts.

I've heard recordings of Buddhist monks chanting. What's that about? Do all Buddhists chant?

Chanting or reciting a mantra is a common practice in some schools of Buddhism, especially in the Tibetan Mahayana tradition. Like meditation, the goal is to break free from the habitual reactivity of thoughts and thinking. When your mind is focused on repeating a mantra or reciting a chant, you have less opportunity to be caught up in habitual thinking and reacting. A mantra is a short phrase or expression, usually in Pali or Sanskrit, that can be repeated over and over. It's not like a prayer, because in Buddhism, there's no deity to direct a prayer to. One of the most common Buddhist chants is *oṃ maṇi padme hūṃ*, which means "jewel in the lotus." Another popular chant is *nam myōhō renge kyō*, which means "I devote myself to the *Lotus Sutra.*"

You're Already Chanting

The first time I heard Buddhist chanting, I thought it was a bit strange. It seemed to me like some mysterious form of worship. But later, when I talked about it with a friend of mine, he pointed out that we're already repeating things to ourselves all the time. Habitual thoughts, like "I'm such an idiot" or "I'm so much better than everyone else," are sorts of mantras that we repeat to ourselves over and over, and they do have an effect over time on how we view ourselves and others. This realization helped me see more value in the practice of reciting mantras or chanting.

One of my favorite mantras to recite is "May I be happy, may I be at peace, and may I be free from suffering." Then I extend that thought out to others—friends, family, even strangers. "May you be happy, may you be at peace, and may you be free from suffering."

Over time, I've become more aware of the regular mantras and expressions that I tend to repeat to myself, which has let me question whether these repetitive thoughts are helpful or not. I've since removed many of the unhealthy repetitive mantras by replacing them with new ones that I've learned. Next time you find yourself repeating an unhelpful thought or series of thoughts to yourself, try redirecting your focus to a positive mantra like the one above.

Some religions use symbols and ritual objects, like the cross or prayer beads. Does Buddhism have things like that?

Several symbols can be found throughout the various schools of Buddhism. Statues of the Buddha are especially common. The Buddha was a man and a teacher rather than a deity, so, with few exceptions, statues of the Buddha are not idols, nor are they worshipped. When Buddhists bow to a statue of the Buddha, it is merely as a sign of reverence. Buddhists treat such images as one might treat an image of a loved one who has passed away. Similarly, Buddhist beads are used for meditation, not prayer. They symbolize unity and harmony: The beads, representing individuals, are held together by a common string, representing the dharma. Buddhist beads are often used to keep count when chanting a mantra, but it's important to note that they're not special or holy. They're simply tools to assist with being more mindful and present.

Other frequently used Buddhist symbols include flowers, candles, incense, and bells, which all help concretize teachings about impermanence and interdependence. Flowers wither and die, candles extinguish, incense diffuses into the great oneness that surrounds it, and the sound of the bell slowly fades until it becomes one with the silence that was there before the bell was struck. As with other Buddhist symbols, these items are powerful metaphorical tools, but they're not special in and of themselves.

What if I'm not interested in Buddhism as a religion or even as a philosophy? I'm just interested in feeling better. Can Buddhist practices help with anxiety and depression?

Yes, they can! Anxiety arises due to the fact that we are capable of imagination, of conjuring up things that don't exist. The same ability that allows us to imagine the future and visualize great outcomes can easily make us worry about difficulties that don't yet exist. When the mind becomes entangled with thoughts about the future, practices like mindfulness meditation can help us become grounded once again in the present moment. The Buddhist approach invites us to greet our anxiety as we would an old friend, rather than resisting or fighting it. Reducing aversion to anxiety has even been clinically shown to reduce the intensity and duration of anxiety attacks.

This goes back to the Buddha's teaching of the two arrows (see page 80). Feelings like anxiety and depression are the first arrow, and the way we feel about these feelings—sad, angry, resentful—is the second arrow. Buddhism teaches us how to avoid this second arrow and thus decrease our suffering.

To study Buddhism, do I need a teacher? How do I find one?

In the past, it was common for students of Buddhism to work with a specific teacher. The dharma was passed on from teacher to student in a continual lineage. This is still common with a lot of schools of Buddhism, but in our day and age, there are also countless books, blogs, videos, articles, podcasts, and many other resources you can find by searching online. Teachers do play an important role in guiding novice students in the right direction, but I believe that this model of teacher/student learning is rapidly evolving. If you're interested in learning from a teacher firsthand, visit a local Buddhist temple and see if it fits well with your learning style. If not, online communities can provide a lot of the same kind of support. As you explore more, keep in mind that the various schools of Buddhism will approach things differently. What works well for one culture or personality may not work well for another. It's not about finding the "right" school of Buddhism—it's about finding the right school of Buddhism for *you*.

You yourself must strive.
The Buddhas only point the way.

THE BUDDHA,
THE DHAMMAPADA

MORE RESOURCES

If you'd like to learn more about Buddhist teachings and concepts, I would recommend the following books.

Buddha by Karen Armstrong

This book is a philosophical biography of the historical figure Siddhartha Gautama (also known as the Buddha). It addresses not just the life of the Buddha but also the world in which he lived and what he did to spawn one of the major world religions.

Buddhism without Beliefs: A Contemporary Guide to Awakening by Stephen Batchelor

This has been one of my longtime go-to books for understanding Buddhist concepts and ideas. The author does a great job of explaining core Buddhist teachings in a pragmatic way.

In the Buddha's Words: An Anthology of Discource from the Pali Canon by Bhikkhu Bodhi

This is my favorite English-language version of the Buddha's sayings, selected from the Pali Canon and translated by an American Buddhist monk.

Beyond Religion and *Ethics for the New Millennium* by the Dalai Lama

The Dalai Lama has written numerous books, but these are two of my favorites. Any reader, Buddhist or not, can gain something valuable from them.

Rebel Buddha: A Guide to a Revolution of Mind by the Dzogchen Ponlop

This book does a good job of explaining the revolutionary process of awakening your own mind, exploring concepts and teachings in a way that is easy to understand.

Buddha's Brain: The Practical Neuroscience of Happiness, Love & Wisdom by Rick Hanson

This book explains the neuroscience that makes our minds work. It does a great job of synthesizing what Buddhism teaches with what we know from neuroscience.

The Center Within by Gyomay Kubose

This book was written by Rev. Gyomay Kubose, whose son, Koyo Kubose, was my teacher. A lot of my understanding of Buddhist concepts and ideas was influenced by the teachings of these two wonderful guides.

Old Path, White Clouds and *The Heart of Understanding* by Thich Nhat Hanh

Like the Dalai Lama, Thich Nhat Hanh has written many excellent books. I think these two are great, accessible starting points for those interested in learning more about Buddhism.

Why Buddhism Is True: The Science and Philosophy of Meditation and Enlightenment by Robert Wright

I like this book because it does a wonderful job of explaining the science behind Buddhism and concrete reasons why Buddhist practices can indeed lead to a more peaceful and joy-filled life.

REFERENCES

"Anuradha Sutta: To Anuradha." Translated by Thanissaro Bhikkhu. Access to Insight. 2004. https://www.accesstoinsight.org /tipitaka/sn/sn22/sn22.086.than.html.

Benedict, Gerald, ed. *Buddhist Wisdom: The Path to Enlightenment.* London: Watkins Publishing, 2009.

Corliss, Julie. "Mindfulness Meditation May Ease Anxiety, Mental Stress." *Harvard Health Blog.* Last modified October 3, 2017. https://www.health.harvard.edu/blog/mindfulness-meditation -may-ease-anxiety-mental-stress-201401086967.

"Cula-Malunkyovada Sutta: The Shorter Instructions to Malunkya." Translated by Thanissaro Bhikkhu. Access to Insight. 1998. https://www.accesstoinsight.org/tipitaka/mn/mn.063.than.html.

The Middle-Length Discourses of the Buddha: A Translation of the Majjhima Nikaya. Translated by Bhikkhu Ñāṇamoli and Bhikkhu Bodhi. Somerville, MA: Wisdom Publications, 2015.

Olendzki, Andrew. *Untangling Self: A Buddhist Investigation of Who We Really Are.* Somerville, MA: Wisdom Publications, 2016.

Rasheta, Noah. "Secular Buddhism with Stephen Batchelor." *Secular Buddhism.* Podcast audio. September 18, 2017. https://secularbuddhism.com/stephen-batchelor/.

"Sallatha Sutta: The Arrow." Translated by Thanissaro Bhikkhu. Access to Insight. 1997. https://www.accesstoinsight.org /tipitaka/sn/sn36/sn36.006.than.html.

Thich Nhat Hanh. *Buddha Mind, Buddha Body.* Berkeley, CA: Parallax Press, 2007.

———. *The Blooming of a Lotus: Guided Meditation for Achieving the Miracle of Mindfulness.* Translated by Annabel Laity. Boston: Beacon Press, 2009.

"Uposatha Sutta: The Observance Day." Translated by John D. Ireland. Access to Insight. 1998. https://www.accesstoinsight .org/tipitaka/kn/ud/ud.5.05.irel.html.

Watts, Alan. *Still the Mind: An Introduction to Meditation.* Novato, CA: New World Library, 2000.

INDEX

A

Abhidhamma Pitaka, 20
Absolute truths, 42–43
Acceptance, 78–79
Action, right, 90
Afterlife, 56–57
Aggregates (skandhas), 98–102
Agnosticism, 64–65
Alcohol, 109, 112
"All-pervasive suffering," 46–47
Ananda, 10, 17
Anattā, 43. *See also* Nonself
Anicca, 43. *See also* Impermanence
Anxiety, 123
Arhat, 24
Atheism, 64–65
Attachment, 52–53
Awakening, 8, 32
Awareness, 38–39, 69, 101

B

Badness, 40–41
Batchelor, Stephen, 72–73
Beads, 122
Beliefs, 64–65, 66
Bodh Gaya, 5
Bodhisattva, 24
Bodhi tree, 5
Budai, 11
Buddha
    death of, 17
    enlightenment of, 4–5, 9
    family of, 10
    as a god, 12
    language of, 3
    meaning of, 8
    name of, 2
    personal appearance of, 11
    philosophy of, 18–19
    statues of, 122
    taking refuge in, 113, 114
    teachings of, 98–101
Buddha-nature, 40–41

Buddhism. *See also specific schools*
    aim of, 14–15
    and anxiety/depression, 123
    and daily life, 68–69
    five precepts, 107–109
    key teaching, 72–73
    and other religions, 66
    as the Path of Liberation, 7
    practicing, 113
    schools of, 22
    symbols and ritual objects, 122
    teachers, 17, 124
    texts and writings, 20–21
    as a way of life, 18–19
    in the West, 27

C

Cause and effect, 62–63
Chanting, 120–121
Communication, 89
Community, 115
Concentration, right, 96
Conceptual truths, 42–43
Consciousness (viññāṇa), 98, 101

D

Dalai Lama, 17, 22, 66
Death, 56–57, 60. *See also* Reincarnation
Depression, 123
Desires, 36
Detachment, 52–53
Dhammapada, 20
Dharma, 2
    taking refuge in, 113, 115
Diamond Sutra, 20
Discipline, right, 94
Distraction, 96
Dukkha, 43. *See also* Suffering

E

Eightfold Path
    ethical conduct, 89–93
    mental discipline, 94–96
    overview, 84–85
    wisdom, 87–88

P

Pali (language), 3, 5, 25
Pali Canon, 3, 10, 20, 25
Parables
    farmer and the horse, 54–55
    poisoned arrow, 18–19, 80, 123
    six blind men and the elephant, 42–43
Path of Liberation, 7. See also Eightfold Path
Perception (sañña), 98, 100
Perceptions
    changing, 97
    of reality, 6–7, 8, 14, 16, 44
    of self, 34, 46–47, 48–49, 50, 52, 98–102
Poisons
    greed, 36
    hatred, 37
    ignorance, 34
Precepts, 107–109
Pure Land Buddhism, 22, 27

R

Reactivity, 80–83
Reality, 6–7, 8, 54, 62–63
Rebirth, 58–59
Reincarnation, 58–59
Religions, 66
Rhaula, 10
Ritual objects, 122

S

Samudaya, 72, 80–81
Sangha (community), taking refuge in, 113, 115
Sanskrit, 3, 5, 8, 25
Self, sense of, 34, 47, 98–102
Sensation (vedanā), 98, 100
Senses, 97, 99
Sexual misconduct, 108
Shakyamuni Buddha, 11
Shakyas, 11
Siddhartha Gautama, 2, 4–5, 10, 11, 17
Skandhas, 98–102
Skillful means, xi
Speech
    incorrect, 109
    right, 89
Statues, 122
Stealing (taking what is not given), 107–108
Subtle impermanence, 44–45

Suffering

Suffering, 14, 33, 34, 37, 43, 46–47
    accepting, 78–79
    embracing, 74–77
    Four Noble Truths, 72–73
    reactivity to, 80–83
"Suffering of loss," 46
"Suffering of suffering," 46
Sutta Pitaka, 20
Symbols, 122

T

Teachers, 124
Tenzin Gyatso, 17
Theism, 64–65, 66
Theravada Buddhism, 20, 22, 24–25, 108
Thich Nhat Hanh, 14, 95
Thought processes, 101
Thoughts, 119
Three marks of existence, 43, 87
"Three poisons"/"three fires," 33–37
"Three refuges"/"three jewels," 113–115
Tibetan Buddhism, 22
Tipitaka, 20. See also Pali Canon
Tisarana, taking refuge in, 113–115
Transcendence, 59
Truth, 42–43

U

Uncertainty, 68
Understanding, right, 87
Universal truths, 43

V

Vajrayana Buddhism, 22, 24–25
Vegetarianism, 111
Vinaya Pitaka, 20

W

Wisdom, 34
Wisdom (pañña), 84–85
    right intent, 88
    right understanding, 87
Worship, 11

Y

Yasodhara, 10

Z

Zazen, 26
Zen Buddhism, 21, 22, 25, 26, 27, 65

ABOUT THE AUTHOR

Noah Rasheta is a Buddhist teacher, lay minister, and author, as well as the host of the podcast *Secular Buddhism*. He teaches mindfulness and Buddhist philosophy online and in workshops all around the world. He works with others to make the world a better place as he studies, embodies, and teaches the fundamentals of Buddhist philosophy, integrating Buddhist teachings with modern science, humanism, and humor. He lives in Kamas, Utah, with his wife and three kids.

CPSIA information can be obtained
at www.ICGtesting.com
Printed in the USA
JSHW011538140323
38926JS00003B/3